"Never has there been more interest in e[...]
everyone wants to know what is going to [...]
world of ours. Bible prophecy and pa[...]
Revelation is the only definitive source [...]
and who better than a distinguished Bible teacher and
phenomenal church builder Pastor Chuck Smith who has
studied and taught the subject for over fifty years. This unique
dramatic treatment is both true to the Scripture and practical,
both hallmarks of all Pastor Chuck's teaching. I found it very
interesting!"

—Tim LaHaye, Co-author of the popular *Left Behind* Series

"When Chuck Smith was born, Israel didn't even exist as a
country. Few Jews lived in the Holy Land. Scarcely anyone on
the planet could envision a day when the Jewish State would
be reborn and dominate global headlines. But the Bible said it
would happen. Chuck Smith believed it would happen. And
then — amazingly, miraculously — it did happen.

"The big question now is: What's next and how should we live
differently in light of the soon coming return of Jesus Christ?
*The Final Act* is a powerful, provocative end times primer and
Chuck Smith — one of America's leading Bible teachers — both
captures the drama, and challenges Christians to study the
script and play their part with passion and courage."

— Joel C. Rosenberg, New York Times best-selling author of
  *Epicenter: Why The Current Rumblings In The Middle East
  Will Change Your Future*

"With his trademark clarity and devotional style, Pastor Chuck
skillfully surveys the key events of the end times and shows how
today's headlines strikingly foreshadow the ancient prophecies of the Bible. *The Final Act* will inform your mind but will
also move your heart to be ready when the curtain goes up."

—Mark Hitchcock, Author of *America in Bible Prophecy,* and
  *The Second Coming of Babylon*

"Chuck Smith's latest book deserves every Christian's serious attention. In it he shows clearly that prophecy, which is unique to the Bible (there are no prophecies in the Qur'an, Hindu Vedas, sayings of Buddha or Confucius, or in any other scriptures of the world's religions), proves both the existence of God and that the Bible is His infallible Word and ought to be heeded by all.

"Chuck provides informative facts, some not generally known. His main focus is upon Israel and the Middle East, and rightly so. That is the subject of most Bible prophecies — in fact, 70 percent of the pages of God's Word.

"Although students of Bible prophecy (there are no 'experts') differ on some of the details (timing of certain events, etc.), there is general agreement that we are in the "last days" and the rapture is very near. The signs are overwhelming, and Chuck does an excellent job of describing current world conditions which support this view. He explains how Israel and the world got to where we are today, where events are headed, and how it all will end.

"I highly recommend *The Final Act* for the careful consideration of every Christian and as a gift for unsaved friends in helping them to come to know Christ."

— Dave Hunt, Co-host of *Search the Scriptures Daily* radio program and author of *America, Israel, and Islam*


"If you've ever wanted a clear and concise picture of the events of the end times then you have your hands on the right book. Chuck Smith has studied and taught prophecy for over fifty years. That in itself is remarkable. But what this book does is to show how all the threads of God's prophetic tapestry are woven together and how it all 'fits' like a seamless garment. Replete with both biblical and historical reference points, *The Final Act* will help you understand who the main characters in the end times are and how events will unfold. I found myself with a renewed excitement for the return of Christ with the turn of every page."

— Skip Heitzig, Host of *Calvary Connection* radio and author of *A Biblical Response to Terror and Confronting your Culture*

"Here is a book on Bible prophecy that everyone can read and understand! The details about what is going on in Israel and the world, plus documentation on past events make this work quite exciting and enjoyable to read. Presenting the future as the 'acts' of a performance or play gives a unique understanding to the reader of what we can expect to occur in our immediate future. In his wonderful conversational style, you feel like the author is talking directly to you as you read this encouraging book. I heartily recommend it and trust that the Lord will use it greatly to draw many people to faith and commitment to our Lord and Savior Jesus Christ. Thank you, Chuck, for putting this one together!"

— David Hocking, Host of the *Hope For Today* radio program and ministries and author of *The Coming World Leader*

*The Final Act* is an exciting, clear explanation of the end times' prophecies. The book seems taken from today's headlines, and even next year's headlines! Pastor Chuck presents (explains) in a simple manner the 'blessed hope' of Jesus' return, and why it may be sooner than we could imagine!"

— Ray Bentley, Host of *In the Word* radio program and author of *God's Pursuing Love*

"I first heard teaching on the subject of Bible prophecy from Pastor Chuck Smith of Calvary Chapel Costa Mesa. It was there that a foundation was laid in my life that I still draw from today.

"Now, everyone can benefit from Chuck's powerful insights from Scripture on this timely topic. *The Final Act* is a practical primer on Bible prophecy. In a systematic yet very understandable way, Chuck lays out the unfolding drama of last days events, step by step. You will have a much clearer understanding of end times' events as a result of reading it. I highly recommend *The Final Act*."

— Greg Laurie, Host of *A New Beginning* radio program and author of *Are We Living in the Last Days?*

chuck smith

# THE

# FINAL

# ACT

**THE WORD**
FOR TODAY

P.O. Box 8000, Costa Mesa, CA 92628 • Web Site: www.twft.com • E-mail: info@twft.com

The Final Act
By Chuck Smith

Published by The Word For Today
P.O. Box 8000 Costa Mesa CA 92628
Web site: http://www.twft.com
(800) 272-WORD (9673)

Printed in the United States of America

# CONTENTS

## Act IV: The Second Coming

# INTRODUCTION

## A Drama In Four Acts

HAVE YOU EVER STOOD DOMINOES on end in a long row? Tip the first domino and the whole line goes down, one right after the other. God is aligning world situations much as we would line up dominoes — and He's getting ready to tip the first event that will trigger a series of events ultimately climaxing in the second coming of Jesus Christ.

What exciting days we are living in! Like observers invited backstage before a play, we can see the director positioning all the players and making sure the props are in order, and we can feel the excitement and drama in these minutes before he signals for the curtain to rise. This analogy is apt, for God is positioning nations and current events before our very eyes. The world is ready for the curtain to be lifted for the final act. Prepare yourself for the drama of the end times — the return of Jesus Christ.

Before we begin to look at world events in light of Bible prophecy, let me emphasize one point. I have no intention of telling you the day that the Lord is coming for His church. I don't know that day. Nobody knows the day or hour (Matthew 24:36), but the Bible does say, "Concerning the times and the seasons, brethren, you have no need that I should write to you. For you yourselves know perfectly that the day of the Lord so comes as a thief in the night. . . . But you, brethren, are not in darkness, so that this day should overtake you as a thief" (1 Thessalonians 5:1–2, 4).

God wants and expects us to be thoroughly aware of the times in which we live. To this end, He gave us in His Word many signs to help us recognize the nearness of His promised return. As Christians, we have the privilege of living in this exciting period and seeing this great drama unfold.

To help us understand these times, *The Final Act* can be viewed as a four-act drama:

**Act I** The stage is set and the plot is introduced. Here we see Israel become a nation, observe the Antichrist, and contemplate escalating world problems.

**Act II** The rapture of the church occurs when God snatches away His people before the great tribulation.

**Act III** The great tribulation is ushered in as God brings judgment upon the world.

**Act IV** The second coming of Christ is witnessed by all as we see Christ judging the earth and setting up His kingdom.

Every good drama concludes with an encore. As *The Final Act* will show you, the Lord's encore is one that will last for eternity.

act I

# SETTING THE
# STAGE

## SCENE 1: Israel

AT FOUR IN THE AFTERNOON, local time, May 14, 1948, David Ben-Gurion proudly pulled himself up to his full height in the crowded Tel Aviv Museum and read these fateful words:

> "It is the self-evident right of the Jewish people to be a nation as all other nations, its own Sovereign State. Accordingly, we meet in solemn assembly today. Thus, by virtue of the natural and historic right of the Jewish people and the Resolution of the General Assembly of the United Nations, we hereby proclaim the establishment of the Jewish State in Palestine to be called the State of Israel."

According to biblical prophecy, Israel's rebirth as a nation sets in motion the rest of the end times' prophecies. Israel's national revival was a vital prop that had to be set on stage before the final act in the drama of man's history could unfold.

Thus, the headliner has taken the stage — Israel in her historic homeland. Two other key players will soon join her under the lights, but before we look at those players, we must first look back to see how God foretold the last days.

## LOOKING BACK TO SEE AHEAD

Daniel is one of the most fascinating books of prophecy in the Bible. The prophet — captured by King Nebuchadnezzar in the first conquest of Israel by the Babylonians — wrote prophecies that give us keen insights into the events that lead to Christ's return.

One night King Nebuchadnezzar had a nightmare that greatly troubled him. He awoke the next morning terrified but unable to remember the details of his dream. The king was left with a lingering sense of horror and a feeling that his dream held a message of critical significance. So he called together all the wise men, astrologers, and soothsayers in the Babylonian kingdom, told them he couldn't recall the details of his nightmare, and ordered them to interpret it for him anyway — under threat of losing their heads if they could not do so.

They couldn't believe Nebuchadnezzar's unreasonable demand. How could they interpret a dream the king himself couldn't remember? Their death seemed inevitable.

Arioch, the captain of the king's guard, told young Daniel of the danger he faced because of the king's decree. Since Daniel was being groomed as a counselor, he too would be executed. He asked the captain to tell the king that there is a God in heaven who knows all things, and that His servant, Daniel, would reveal the dream's meaning. Arioch told Nebuchadnezzar of the young Hebrew captive Daniel, who served a God who could answer the king's request.

Meanwhile Daniel went to his friends and told them to pray that God might reveal the king's dream to them. God was faithful and revealed both the dream and its interpretation. Nebuchadnezzar quickly summoned Daniel and told him he'd heard that Daniel could tell him his dream and interpret its meaning.

Daniel answered, "No, I can't. But there is a God in heaven who knows all things. He knows what you dreamed and what it means, and He has revealed it to me." Then he continued, "The other night, O King Nebuchadnezzar, as you were lying on your bed, you were thinking of the power and greatness of your Babylonian kingdom. Then the thought came into your mind, 'What shall come to pass in the future? What will happen to my kingdom? How will the world end?' So God gave you a dream in which He has revealed to you what will take place in the last days.

"In your dream you saw a great image. It had a head of gold, breast and arms of silver, stomach and thighs of brass, legs of iron, and feet of iron and clay with ten toes. You watched the image until a stone not cut with hands hit the great image in its feet. The image crumbled and the stone grew into a mountain that filled the entire earth." At that moment Nebuchadnezzar recalled the dream that Daniel described and pressed him to explain its meaning.

Daniel explained, "You, O king, are the head of gold. God has given you a great and powerful kingdom which has extended throughout the civilized earth. After you, another kingdom shall rise that is inferior to you."

In Daniel 8:20, this kingdom is identified as the Medo-Persian Empire which, under Cyrus, did indeed conquer Babylon. However, as the interpretation continued, this kingdom was also to be supplanted by the kingdom represented by the brass stomach, identified in Daniel 8:21 as Greece. This is a fascinating prophecy indeed, for at this time (approximately 600 BC) Greece was a small, almost unknown province in the western part of the world.

The kingdom of Greece was to be conquered by the kingdom represented by the iron legs which, historically, turned out to be the Roman Empire. Rome was as strong as iron, and it broke and subdued the world under its iron fist. So far these predictions have unfolded in an easily traceable historical sequence. But we are left with a prediction of a final world-dominating kingdom not specifically identified and not yet exercising its rule over the earth. Since the time of the Roman Empire, there has not been a power that dominated the entire world.

From the description of its makeup as part iron and part clay, inasmuch as the iron represented imperial Rome, the final kingdom will be related to the Roman Empire. The fact that it is mixed with clay indicates that it will be weaker than iron alone. This could possibly signify a weak attempt at reviving imperial Rome. We are told that the ten toes represent ten kings that shall unite their power.

When Nebuchadnezzar heard Daniel's interpretation of his dream, he acknowledged that indeed there was no god in all the world like the God of Daniel (Daniel 2:47).

Later though, Nebuchadnezzar defied the revelation of God and ordered a great image ninety feet high made entirely of gold to be erected in the plain of Dura. By making it all gold, Nebuchadnezzar was declaring that no one would conquer his kingdom and that Babylon would stand forever. The king ordered all the people to bow down and worship this golden image under threat of death. This is where the story of the three young Hebrew men, Shadrach, Meshach, and Abednego comes in. For refusing to bow to the image, they were cast into a burning furnace. There in the flames, a fourth man with the likeness of the Son of God joined them and protected them from being harmed by the fire (Daniel 3:25, 27). The question arises, where was Daniel at the time that his close friends were going through this ordeal? We must assume that he either bowed down to the image (which is very unlikely) or that he was out of the country at the time. This story contains a fascinating analogy, for Scripture tells us that the Antichrist is going to set up an image in the last days and demand that mankind bow to it or be put to death (Revelation 13:15). The three Hebrews are a type of the 144,000 Jews that the Lord will seal to preserve them through this time of fiery judgment (Revelation 7:1–8). Daniel's absence may be a type of the church which will be mysteriously gone during the great tribulation.

After this, Nebuchadnezzar went insane and lived and ate with the wild oxen in the fields. His hair grew long and covered his body like feathers, and his nails became like claws. He took total leave of his senses until seven seasons passed over him. It is unclear whether "seven seasons" refers to seven years or seven literal seasons, such as winter, spring, summer, and fall. Nebuchadnezzar could have been in this state of insanity for one-and-three-quarters years or for as long as seven years. Regardless of the length of his insanity, he remained in this condition long enough to know that the God of heaven lifts up and establishes kings and pulls down those whom He chooses. The king, then, acknowledged the power of God until the end of his life (Daniel 4:31–37).

During the first year of King Belshazzar's reign, approximately seventy years after Nebuchadnezzar's dream, Daniel had a vision. In it, he saw a bear with three ribs in its mouth devour a lion with the wings of an eagle. The bear was then destroyed by a leopard; which in turn was broken in pieces and trampled on by a fierce, dreadful beast with ten horns. An eleventh horn rose up and destroyed three others. This horn then became a great power, and spoke blasphemous things. In many ways, Daniel's vision paralleled Nebuchadnezzar's dream. The four animals in Daniel's vision represent the same world-governing empires as the metals of the image in the king's dream.

Looking at history, we can see that these prophecies of Daniel have been fulfilled. The Babylonian Empire (represented by the head of gold, or lion) was overthrown by the Medo-Persians (breast of silver, or bear); the Medo-Persian Empire was quickly conquered by the Greeks (stomach of brass, or leopard); and the Grecian Empire thereafter came under the control of the Romans (legs of iron, or indescribable beast) (Daniel 7:1–8).

This prophecy could easily be embodied by the nations of Europe that are presently binding themselves together with economic treaties, known as the treaty of Rome, for the purpose of forming a United States of Europe or a much more powerful version of the European Economic Community (EEC). All of the economic borders within the EEC nations were removed at midnight, December, 1992. A common European currency already exists and may supplant individual monetary systems. We are just beginning to realize the awesome ramifications of this economic world giant.

The exciting aspect of this whole prophecy to Bible believers is found in Daniel 2:44, where we are told that it is during the days of these kings that the God of heaven will come to establish His kingdom. This Rock which is "not cut with human hands" is Jesus Christ, who is coming again to establish God's everlasting kingdom.

Now that the stage has been set and these prophecies fulfilled, what about more recent history? What has happened in recent years, and what is going on today?

## ISRAEL IN THE 20TH CENTURY

In October 1973, during Yom Kippur (the holiest day of the year for the Jews), Syria and Egypt simultaneously attacked Israel from opposite ends of the country. The majority of the Israelis — including regular army personnel — were either in their synagogues or resting quietly at home. In respect of the Yom Kippur, communication networks had been silent all day. Suddenly, sirens began wailing in Tel Aviv and Jerusalem. Radios came alive with emergency code numbers for the nation's military troops, and calls went out to reservists to activate and defend themselves.

The Syrians and Egyptians had launched what was intended to be the "war of annihilation." Twelve hundred

Syrian tanks attacked the Golan Heights in an initial assault over a twenty-mile area. (To give you some perspective on that, when Hitler made his major invasion of the Soviet Union in World War II, he used one thousand tanks over a two-hundred-mile perimeter.) In the Sinai, Egypt attacked with three thousand tanks and one thousand pieces of major artillery. The battle was intended to completely destroy the nation of Israel, and the unified Arab powers almost achieved their goal. Were it not for miracles far greater than those that took place during the 1967 war, Israel would not be a nation today. When this Arab confederacy attacked Israel with vast superiority in both numbers and weaponry, miracles like those in the Bible occurred.

From this near disaster rose many stories of bravery and personal heroism. As Zechariah prophesied, some of the insignificant soldiers became as David (Zechariah 12:8). Consider the case of Lieutenant Zvi Greengold, a man who would come to be known by the nickname "Zwicka." Lieutenant Greengold was with his family at Kibbutz Lochamei Hagetaot when the war broke out. He immediately put on his uniform, hitchhiked to the headquarters at Nafech on the Golan front, and asked for a tank command. Only three tanks were available — and two were damaged and heading in for repairs. So Lieutenant Greengold took the third and headed out. He quickly found himself in the thick of battle. He managed to knock out several Syrian tanks but in the meantime saw his own support tanks go down. Realizing he'd have to leave the main road to survive, he began maneuvering from behind the knolls that parallel the highway. Zwicka would come up over a small hill, destroy one of the Syrian tanks, then race back behind the hilly ground and repeat his action. He knocked out so many tanks that the Syrians thought they were facing a whole Israeli tank brigade! Believing themselves to be outmanned, they retreated.

With odds of fifty to one against him, Zwicka turned back the Syrian attack that day. After each successful strike, he radioed back to headquarters that "the Zwicka unit had destroyed another Syrian tank," leading headquarters to think that Zwicka was a whole armored unit. But this brave soldier was out there all alone, holding off the Syrian advance. His is only one of countless stories of David-like heroism to come out of the Yom Kippur War.

The Syrians easily poured through the southern section of the Golan Heights where Israeli defenses had been depleted, and actually came within one mile of the headquarters of the Israeli Army. At the time the Syrians approached this base of operations, the Israelis had only two tanks and ten men to defend the headquarters. It seems strange that wave after wave of Syrian tanks moved in, but stopped a mile from this strategic outpost. Later, the Golan Heights commander laughed and said the Syrians had an excellent view of the Sea of Galilee and stopped to admire it. He confessed that he really didn't know why they stopped their unrestrained advance.

It is speculated that since the Syrians weren't able to move through the northern sector, they may have suspected that the Israelis were letting them pour freely through on the south in order to trap them. The Syrians didn't know that on the first day of the war they could have moved all the way to Tiberias. They could have taken the whole Galilee region.

Down in the Sinai, the Egyptians were planning to take the Bar-Lev line within twenty-four hours. They took it in just five hours, and were so surprised with their quick success that they decided to wait there. They had no contingency plans for moving further so soon, and were unaware that the only obstacles between them and Tel Aviv were ninety battered Israeli tanks. Mysteriously, both the Syrians and the Egyptians halted long enough to give the Israelis a chance to mobilize their reserve units and counterattack both in the Golan Heights and in the Sinai.

When the Israelis began their assault in the Golan Heights, they pushed the Syrians back until Israeli tank units came within twelve miles of Damascus. Israel then brought in its artillery units to bombard the Syrian capital. In a brilliant move in the Sinai, General Ariel Sharon crossed the Suez Canal with an assault force and trapped the entire Egyptian Third Army on the Sinai Peninsula — making the Egyptians completely dependent upon the Israelis for their food and medicine.

Just hours after the war began, Soviet Premier Leonid Brezhnev cabled U.S. President Richard Nixon and told him that the Soviet Union would begin unilateral action to bring an enforced "peace" to the Middle East. Ironically, Soviet cargo planes were on their way to the region before the war ever started. As early as October 6, 1973, Russian ships landed in Alexandria, Egypt, and in the Syrian port of Latakia with war supplies.

Three days before hostilities began the USSR sent up spy satellites designed to photograph and monitor Israel. The Arab attack was originally scheduled for 6:00 P.M. on Yom Kippur, but satellite data showed the Israelis had begun to mobilize, so the attack was moved ahead by four hours. Because Syria didn't have enough trained personnel, Soviet soldiers manned some of the invading tanks, and many Soviet soldiers were captured by the Israelis on the Golan Heights, a fact which was later hushed up.

I was in Israel during the Yom Kippur War. On my way from Tel Aviv to my hotel in Bat Yom, I talked with my cab driver, who told me that he was a lieutenant in the army and I was his last fare before he reported for duty. I told him I'd be praying for him because this time it looked as if the war would be a tough one.

He said, "Yes, it is. We're fighting the Russians this time."

I agreed and said, "The Russians have moved in some advanced equipment. The SAM-6's are really potent missiles. You're fighting against sophisticated Russian weapons this time."

He said, "I didn't say Russian weapons. We're fighting against the Russians. We've already captured several of them in the Golan Heights."

The capture of Russian personnel in the Golan Heights was reported in *Time* magazine, then mysteriously hushed.

In a single air battle in the Sinai, five Russian MIGs were shot down. All five were piloted by Red Army personnel. The Soviets had moved a heavy cruiser with nuclear warheads on its decks into Alexandria. This was spotted by U.S. reconnaissance.

When Brezhnev notified President Nixon that the USSR would take unilateral action to bring peace to the Middle East, he was really saying that they were preparing to invade Israel. The war had started to turn against Egypt and Syria. In fact, Russia reassigned their cargo planes and loaded them with Soviet paratroopers. The Red Army had full intentions to launch a paratroop attack against Israel.

When the Soviets took over Czechoslovakia during the rebellion in 1968, the first thing they did was to send in paratroopers to take over the airport. Once Red Army troops captured the airport and sealed it off, they immediately brought in their supplies and tanks and were able to move from the heart of the country to put down the rebellion. It's a typical Soviet tactic of warfare.

Therefore, when Brezhnev cabled the threat to Nixon, the President put U.S. troops on alert around the world. U.S. Secretary of State, Henry Kissinger began fast-paced trips from Israel to Syria to Cairo in an effort to hammer out a quick cease-fire before the Russians moved in. For a moment, World War III loomed. We came close to seeing the end in 1973, but God had other purposes. He brought the war to a halt.

Looking back, the Israelis feel they made a mistake in halting their advance, which robbed them of a full and decisive victory over the Arabs. They could have fired on Damascus with their tanks, forcing the city to surrender. General Sharon pleaded for permission to move against Cairo while he had the momentum going with him, leaving the Egyptian army trapped and helpless. But U.S. pressure stopped him and kept the Jews from total victory.

In 1982 it became apparent that the Soviet Union was again planning to aid an attack on Israel. Many Israeli military officers believe that the move by the Israeli army into southern Lebanon in June of that year thwarted a planned fall invasion. As the Israeli Army moved north during Operation Peace for Galilee, they discovered a vast and amazing store of weapons. Prime Minister Menachem Begin declared that even though Israeli Intelligence was one of the best in the world and knew that weapons were being stored in southern Lebanon, the amount of weapons captured was ten times greater than had been expected. Using more than a score of huge truck-and-trailer rigs operating twenty-four hours a day, it took over three months to transfer these weapons back to Israel. They also captured four hundred new T-62 tanks, the plans for the proposed invasion, and enough weapons to equip three army divisions. The only place where you could find enough trained personnel to use such a large store of weapons would have been the Soviet Union.

Syria has only increased her arsenal of weapons in the years since the Yom Kippur War. Some sources say that it has tripled its strength. Over twelve hundred Russian advisors have instructed the Iraqis in the use of thousands of tanks, planes and the now famous Scud Missile which the Soviets supplied. One intelligence source has said that Iraq has stored many of her weapons of mass destruction in Syria. We do know that the Syrians, as well as Iran, have armed Hezbollah in Lebanon. Not only that, but Al Qaeda cells are being developed and are proliferating in Lebanon.

## ISRAELI ATTITUDE CHANGING

In AD 72, when the Roman general Silvanus was making his final assault against the elevated city of Masada, the 960 Jewish inhabitants watched the Roman soldiers putting the finishing touches to a tremendous ramp they'd been building at the rear of their fortress. Those Jewish hold-outs knew that in the morning the Romans would attack and they would not be able to hold off the assault. Ben Eleazar called the people together in the synagogue and announced that they would either see their wives ravaged before their eyes, or they could take the honorable way out and commit mass suicide. Rather than submit to slavery, the people chose suicide.

Lots were drawn and ten men were chosen to go through the city of Masada and systematically kill the children first, then the wife, and then the husband of each family. As each family was visited, the husband and wife would kiss their children, and then each other, good-bye. Then, lying on the floor, their throats were slit.

When the work was finished, the surviving ten men gathered in a room and drew lots again to determine who would be the last to die. As nine men lay on the floor, the man chosen to die last slit their throats. And when they were all dead, he then committed suicide.

When the Romans broke into the city of Masada the following morning, they were horrified to discover what had transpired in the night. All the city's inhabitants were dead, with the exception of one old lady and a few children who had hidden in a cave. Rome had conquered Masada — but theirs was an empty victory.

The belief shown by these Jews — the belief that suicide is better than slavery — is known as the "Masada Complex." Prior to the 1973 war, this was the feeling of most Jews in Israel. In fact, until just recently, Jewish military cadets were taken to Masada for their graduation exercises. The leaders would recount the story of Masada and then the group as a whole would declare together, "Masada shall not fall again." What they were saying, in essence, was that they agreed with the statement made by those long-ago resisters, and they, too, promised to fight until they die.

However, attitudes in Israel are changing. A new attitude is slowly replacing the Masada Complex — the "Samson Complex." Samson also committed suicide, but when he did, he took his enemies with him. When he knew his time was short, Samson had a little boy lead him to the main support pillars of the temple of his Philistine captors. Samson then bowed with all his strength, and as the Spirit of the Lord came upon him, he pulled the pillars together and collapsed the temple. Samson died — but three thousand Philistines were crushed along with him (Judges 16:26–30). Today some Israeli leaders say that if they have to go, they'll take the world with them. They feel — with good reason — that the world has let them down.

When, during the Yom Kippur War, Israel came close to running out of ammunition, the United States could not help because Germany, England, Italy, and France refused to let U.S. supply planes land and refuel on their soil. After ten days, Portugal finally opened up a base on the Azores for refueling. U.S. planes were soon landing almost nose-to-tail at the Ben Gurion International Airport, re-supplying the Israeli army just in time to keep them ahead in the war.

Perhaps with this event lingering in their minds, Israelis feel that Europe has deserted her. The unspoken attitude is, "If we fall, why should we care if the world also falls?"

Without a doubt, Israel will defend themselves in future conflicts with every resource available to them. And they have the right to do so.

## AN ISRAELI PERSPECTIVE TODAY

In September 2006, Professor Arieh Eldad was invited to come to an evening service at Calvary Chapel Costa Mesa and share his views on how Israel should respond to the dilemma they face with the nuclear threat from Iran, the emboldened Hezbollah, and with militant Islam threatening Israel's existence with Russia's support.

Professor Eldad is a sitting member of the Knesset — the Israeli Parliament, as well as the head of the Knesset's Ethics committee — a man who has been hailed by the Israeli press as an honest, hardworking lawmaker. He is a professor, a Brigadier General in the Israeli Defense Force (IDF), and the head of Plastic Surgery in the burns unit at the Hadassah Medical Center in Jerusalem. Dr. Eldad, a recipient of the Evans Award from the American Burns Treatment Association, is known worldwide for his treatment of burns.

Lastly, Professor Eldad is a Revisionist Zionist. Simply stated, he supports the right of Jews to live in any part of the land of Israel they choose, and opposes any surrender of Israeli sovereignty to the Palestine Liberation Organization (PLO). He also opposes the creation of any Palestinian Arab state west of the Jordan River, a possibility he believes would be disastrous.

Here are Professor Eldad's remarks:

"In the year 2000, after an almost twenty-year presence in Southern Lebanon, Israel evacuated this area and hoped for peace and serenity on her northern border. In July of this year, after terrorists from the Hezbollah organization crossed the border into Israel, killed eight IDF soldiers and kidnapped two others, war broke out in Lebanon and Northern Israel. During the past six years, due to the strategic blindness of her leaders, Israel allowed the Hezbollah to equip themselves with 15,000 missiles of various ranges, products of Syria, Iran, Russia and China, and to establish a vast system of underground bunkers underneath the cover of residential homes, mosques, and schools. For the first time in Israeli history, the results were not a clear victory.

"Meanwhile, along the border between Israel and the Gaza Strip, Arab terrorist organizations have been firing thousands of rockets at Israeli towns. During this entire period, weapons, ammunition, and explosives were smuggled into Gaza via the Sinai Peninsula of Egypt. It was from this area that Israel withdrew during the 'disengagement' plan exactly a year ago. Israel had hoped for peace and quiet as a result of this step, and in return received an unending war. The strategic political blindness that led to disengagement has incurred harsh terror attacks which continue to this day.

"Military experts and experts on Islam say that there is no correlation between these two fronts. The Hamas is a Sunni terror organization. Its headquarters is situated in Damascus, Syria. The Hezbollah, which fights Israel from Lebanon, is a Shiite organization which receives its funding, equipment, and training from Iran.

"Sometimes the experts, who know too many details, lose sight of the overall picture. Certainly there is a difference between Sunni and Shiites, between Syria and Iran. However, they are united in their goal of exterminating Israel.

"The war is not about 'occupied territories' or about settlements. The war is against the very fact of the existence of the State of Israel as the homeland for the Jewish people, in the Holy Land. Israel withdrew from Southern Lebanon and the Gaza Strip, and the Arabs turned these areas immediately into giant terror bases. In the eyes of the Arabs, Tel Aviv is a settlement exactly like Beit El, Shiloh or my home in Kfar Adumim. The Arabs want everything and they want us dead. Terror itself is not as dangerous as the tendency of Israel leaders in recent years to capitulate and withdraw. These withdrawals only encouraged terrorists to redouble their efforts to harm Israel. Iran entered into the equation in the last decade. The latest war in Lebanon was not between Israel and the Hezbollah. It was between Israel and an Iranian front unit.

"What does Iran want from us?

"For those who are not familiar with the map of the Middle East, Iran is not situated on the border of Israel. The distance between the two countries is almost 1,000 miles. Iran has no territorial or political demands from Israel. In spite of this, Iran decided that she must destroy

Israel. Iran has developed a massive industry for the enrichment of uranium for the purpose of creating nuclear weapons. She has developed long-range missiles capable of reaching Israel, and Iran's nuclear program is advancing rapidly. In order to prevent Israel from taking military action against her, Iran is using her Syrian ally to advance the goals of the terrorist organizations Hezbollah and Hamas, in order to embroil Israel in unending warfare, and to demonstrate that the moment Israel tries to militarily strike at Iran, the entire civilian population of Israel would be exposed to attack by thousands of missiles and rockets already situated in Southern Lebanon and Gaza, thus effectively preventing Israel from going to war against Iran at all.

"Many Israelis, like most of the Western world, really do not understand what motivates Iran. For the last forty years, we were brainwashed, along with Europe and America, into believing that the problem is the 'occupation', the 'refugees of 1948', or various other border disputes. Having become desperate in the failure of the attempts through conventional warfare, Iran set out to destroy Israel. Those who are familiar with the Bible will recall that this is not the first time that a plan to destroy Israel has originated in Persia. It is worth recalling that the first plan for the 'Final Solution for the Jewish People' in the world did not come from Nazi Germany. Twenty-five hundred years earlier, as we read in the Book of Esther (beginning 3:8 and onward), says Haman, the senior minister of Persian the king, Achashverosh:

"'There is a certain people scattered abroad and dispersed among the people in all the provinces of thy kingdom and their laws are different from all the people; nor do they keep the king's laws; therefore it is of no benefit to the king to tolerate them, if it please the king let it be written that they may be destroyed. . . . And the letters were sent by couriers to all the king's provinces, to destroy, to kill, and to annihilate all Jews, both young and old, little children and women, in one day.'

"Today there is still a window of opportunity to exert massive political pressure on Iran in order to stop the enrichment of uranium. However, the chances for succeeding in this effort are slim. The available time remaining is passing quickly. Iran is also developing long-range missiles in order to deter America from intervening militarily against Iran. The threat is against the entire free world. However, similar to the time of Hitler, the international community hesitates to bear arms and to fight for its survival.

"Ahmadinejad and his plans must be eliminated physically — this year and not next year — as next year may be too late. Whoever hopes that diplomatic international pressure will cause Iran to retreat from its plans does not fully grasp the motivations that are at work. It goes against our rationality. Ahmadinejad sees himself as the leader of the Moslem Crusade against Western culture, as represented by Israel and America. We are in the middle of the third world war — what happened on 9/11 is just a part of this war.

"If Europe will not enlist in this war, then it will be the responsibility of the U.S. and Israel to do the job of protecting the whole world. If Israel finds itself alone, then it will act at all costs. We did not return to our promised land just to turn it into a big concentration site which will allow the enemies of Israel to destroy all the Jews at the press of a button.

"Israel will have to fight in the Gaza Strip, Syria and Lebanon. And then, after we have secured the home front, Israel — and if there is no other alternative — Israel alone, can attack Iran in order to destroy their nuclear weapons program. These are the challenges facing Israel, and in order to accomplish this, we will have to change the Israeli leadership which has failed in the last war. We need your help in order not to stand alone in opposing all of these enemies. Then we can go to battle carrying in our hearts the prayer of our King David, from Psalms chapter 83:

"'Do not keep silence, O God; do not hold thy peace, and be not still O God. For lo, thy enemies make a tumult; and they who hate thee have lifted up their head. They take crafty counsel against thy people, and consult against thy hidden ones. They have said, Come and let us cut them off from being a nation; that the name of Yisrael may be no more in remembrance. For they have consulted together with one consent: they are confederate against thee; the tents of Edom, and the Yishmeelim' of Moav, and the Hagrim . . . Ashur also is joined with them . . . O my God, make them like the whirling chaff; like the stubble before the wind. As the fire burns

41

the wood, and the flame sets the mountains on fire, so pursue them with thy tempest and terrify them with thy storm ... That men may know that thou alone, whose name is the Lord, art the most high over all the earth.'" [1]

## ISRAEL'S NUCLEAR POTENTIAL

It is a well-known fact that Israel possesses nuclear weapons. Israel does not attempt to keep this a secret. In the past, when threatened by Iraq, Israel declared that if Iraq used weapons of mass destruction against them, Israel would unleash the full force of her capabilities against Iraq. We can assume the same would hold true for all her enemies. Professor Eldad said as much in his comments above: *"If Israel finds itself alone, then it will act at all costs."* Israel has often declared that her greatest problem is that she can't afford to lose. To that end, Israel has continued to develop and increase its nuclear capabilities.

As evidence of Israel's willingness to use nuclear weapons, it was reported that during the very crucial moments early in the 1973 war, when it looked as if Israel would be defeated, they took steps to begin activating some of their

---

[1] Maranatha Prophecy Conference DVD, (The Word for Today, 2006). Used by permission.

nuclear bombs. And as early as 1977 there were indica-
tions that Israel possessed a neutron bomb, a weapon
the United States was still developing at the time. The
neutron bomb is that great "humanitarian weapon" that
destroys people but doesn't destroy buildings or indus-
tries. It is designed to kill by ultrahigh radiation.

In his book *Hiroshima,* John Hersey describes the effects
of the atomic bomb dropped on Hiroshima, Japan
during World War II. Many people survived the initial
blast but died from the effects of radiation. He describes
how eyeballs melted and poured down people's faces.
Sores that would not heal broke out upon their bodies,
and their flesh dissolved as a result of exposure to high
radiation.[2] The effects of radiation on people from the
bomb explosion in Hiroshima are identical to those the
neutron bomb is designed to cause. The prospect of the
use of this weapon is horrifying.

In this light, Zechariah 14:12 becomes very interesting.
After speaking about the rebirth of the nation of Israel,
Zechariah describes the after-effects of a war with her sur-
rounding enemies. "And this shall be the plague with which
the LORD will strike all the people who fought against Jerusalem: their flesh shall dissolve while they stand on their

---

[2] John R. Hersey, *Hiroshima,* p. 68 (New York: Random House,
Inc., 1946).

feet, their eyes shall dissolve in their sockets, and their tongues shall dissolve in their mouths."

To me, that sounds like death from severe radiation. And Ezekiel 39 appears to back this up. In verses 1-10, God describes the demise of Gog:

> THUS SAYS THE LORD GOD: BEHOLD, I AM AGAINST YOU, O GOG, THE PRINCE OF ROSH, MESHECH, AND TUBAL; AND I WILL TURN YOU AROUND AND LEAD YOU ON, BRINGING YOU UP FROM THE FAR NORTH, AND BRING YOU AGAINST THE MOUNTAINS OF ISRAEL. THEN I WILL KNOCK THE BOW OUT OF YOUR LEFT HAND, AND CAUSE THE ARROWS TO FALL OUT OF YOUR RIGHT HAND. YOU SHALL FALL UPON THE MOUNTAINS OF ISRAEL, YOU AND ALL YOUR TROOPS AND THE PEOPLES WHO *ARE* WITH YOU; I WILL GIVE YOU TO BIRDS OF PREY OF EVERY SORT AND *TO* THE BEASTS OF THE FIELD TO BE DEVOURED. YOU SHALL FALL ON THE OPEN FIELD; FOR I HAVE SPOKEN, SAYS THE LORD GOD. AND I WILL SEND FIRE ON MAGOG AND ON THOSE WHO LIVE IN SECURITY IN THE COASTLANDS. THEN THEY SHALL KNOW THAT I *AM* THE LORD. SO I WILL MAKE MY HOLY NAME KNOWN IN THE MIDST OF MY PEOPLE ISRAEL,

AND I WILL NOT *LET THEM* PROFANE MY HOLY NAME ANYMORE. THEN THE NATIONS SHALL KNOW THAT I *AM* THE LORD, THE HOLY ONE IN ISRAEL. SURELY IT IS COMING, AND IT SHALL BE DONE, SAYS THE LORD GOD. THIS IS THE DAY OF WHICH I HAVE SPOKEN.

THEN THOSE WHO DWELL IN THE CITIES OF ISRAEL WILL GO OUT AND SET ON FIRE AND BURN THE WEAPONS, BOTH THE SHIELDS AND BUCKLERS, THE BOWS AND ARROWS, THE JAVELINS AND SPEARS; AND THEY WILL MAKE FIRES WITH THEM FOR SEVEN YEARS. THEY WILL NOT TAKE WOOD FROM THE FIELD NOR CUT DOWN *ANY* FROM THE FORESTS, BECAUSE THEY WILL MAKE FIRES WITH THE WEAPONS; AND THEY WILL PLUNDER THOSE WHO PLUNDERED THEM, AND PILLAGE THOSE WHO PILLAGED THEM, SAYS THE LORD GOD.

The Lord then describes the condition of the bodies left in the valley:

IT WILL COME TO PASS IN THAT DAY *THAT* I WILL GIVE GOG A BURIAL PLACE THERE IN ISRAEL, THE VALLEY OF THOSE WHO PASS BY EAST OF THE SEA; AND IT WILL OBSTRUCT TRAVELERS,

BECAUSE THERE THEY WILL BURY GOG AND ALL HIS MULTITUDE. THEREFORE THEY WILL CALL *IT* THE VALLEY OF HAMON GOG. FOR SEVEN MONTHS THE HOUSE OF ISRAEL WILL BE BURYING THEM, IN ORDER TO CLEANSE THE LAND. INDEED ALL THE PEOPLE OF THE LAND WILL BE BURYING, AND THEY WILL GAIN RENOWN FOR IT ON THE DAY THAT I AM GLORIFIED, SAYS THE LORD GOD. THEY WILL SET APART MEN REGULARLY EMPLOYED, WITH THE HELP OF A SEARCH PARTY, TO PASS THROUGH THE LAND AND BURY THOSE BODIES REMAINING ON THE GROUND, IN ORDER TO CLEANSE IT. AT THE END OF SEVEN MONTHS THEY WILL MAKE A SEARCH. THE SEARCH PARTY WILL PASS THROUGH THE LAND; AND *WHEN ANYONE* SEES A MAN'S BONE, HE SHALL SET UP A MARKER BY IT, TILL THE BURIERS HAVE BURIED IT IN THE VALLEY OF HAMON GOG. *THE* NAME OF *THE* CITY *WILL* ALSO *BE* HAMONAH. THUS THEY SHALL CLEANSE THE LAND.

God specifically says that for a period of seven months, no one will touch the bones of these victims. Instead, whenever they come across a body, they'll mark its location with a flag. Eventually, professional buriers will be hired to bury the carcasses. Could the refusal to touch these remains be caused by fear of radioactive contamination?

Twenty-five hundred years ago, God described a plague remarkably similar to the effects of the intense radiation of a neutron bomb. I can't say that's exactly how Israel will defeat the Russian alliance, but certainly the description in Zechariah raises some interesting possibilities.

## A HEAVY STONE

Both Ezekiel and Zechariah prophesied about the rebirth of Israel in the last days. In Ezekiel 37:12, God said, "Therefore prophesy and say to them, 'Thus says the Lord GOD: Behold, O My people, I will open your graves and cause you to come up from your graves, and bring you into the land of Israel.'" He likened Israel to the dry, scattered bones of a forgotten skeleton, lying in the desert. After 2,000 years of exile, God would draw those bones together and cover them with muscle and sinew and flesh. He'd breathe life into them again, and bring them back into the land.

But then, Ezekiel continues, after they are restored in their homeland and dwelling in safety, an evil thought will enter the mind of the leader of Magog who will join with Muslim nations to destroy Jerusalem. At that time, Iran, Persia, Ethiopia, and Libya will unite against Jerusalem.

This scenario is echoed in the twelfth chapter of Zechariah, where God told the prophet that His people would come back into the land of Israel and inhabit Jerusalem again. But in that day, Jerusalem would become a heavy stone or "burdensome" to all of her neighbors round about. It should come as no surprise to us that Israel exists in a circle of hostility. Scripture prophesied of these ongoing conflicts long before the nation's rebirth.

In that same passage, God promised that even though all the nations of the world would gather against her (and we see that happening today), God would defend the inhabitants of Jerusalem, and that the feeblest among them "shall be like David" (Zechariah 12:2–9).

When you look at the prophesies in Ezekiel and Zechariah, and then you look at the gathering storm around Israel, the clear conclusion is that we are living in the last days. At virtually any moment, the Middle East could erupt into a final conflict that will escalate into the "war of annihilation." When that happens, Israel will use every force available to her — including nuclear weaponry. Undoubtedly, such action would elicit a swift response from Russia.

Scripture tells us clearly that at some point, Russia will move against Israel. When this happens, the final countdown will begin. We will then be at the scene that God described in Ezekiel 38 and 39. Russia's invasion of Israel is the first event that will trigger a sequence of events during the final seven years: the emergence of the ten-nation European power, the rise of the Antichrist, the great tribulation during the last half of the seven years, and then the coming of Jesus Christ with His church in power and glory! Finally, the world will see the establishment of God's kingdom, which will bring everlasting righteousness.

## THE RUSSIAN THREAT

The Bible predicts a ten-nation European confederacy will rise to power and become the last world-governing empire. However, Russia presents a major stumbling block to this European Union (EU) becoming a world-governing power. The EU cannot rise to predicted prominence as long as the Russian alliance poses such a tremendous threat to the European continent.

Many of our military strategists believe that because of its vast superiority of personnel and conventional weaponry, Russia could conquer all of Western Europe in seven days — *without the use of nuclear weapons.*

Sounds like a formidable foe. But the situation is well in hand. God has a unique plan to take care of Russia.

How will God remove the Russian alliance as a major military threat? How will ten European nations become a world power? And how will the Antichrist take over as the leader of these ten nations and bring the world under his power? The answers are found in the prophecies of Ezekiel.

As mentioned previously, God showed Ezekiel a valley of dry bones — a vision of the glorious resurrection of the nation of Israel. After foretelling the nation's rebirth, God then laid out the events that would transpire after Israel had resettled in the land and were dwelling in peace.

> THUS SAYS THE LORD GOD: ON THAT DAY IT SHALL COME TO PASS THAT THOUGHTS WILL ARISE IN YOUR MIND, AND YOU WILL MAKE AN EVIL PLAN (EZEKIEL 38:10).

Throughout history, Magog has been known as that vast area north of the Caucasus Mountains. Today we call it Russia. God continued, "Gomer and all its troops; the house of Togarmah from the far north and all its troops — many people are with you" (Ezekiel 38:6). God even listed the nations that would be allied with the Russian alliance. In most cases, the countries God listed are within the Russian sphere of influence today. In a recently formed alliance, Iran has sided with Russia against Israel. Turkey, or Togarmah as named in Ezekiel, has elected a fundamentalist Islamic president who is looking to break ties with the West, that Turkey might become allied with the Islamic nations.

God then said, "I will turn you around, put hooks into your jaws, and lead you out, with all your army, horses, and horsemen, all splendidly clothed, a great company with bucklers and shields, all of them handling swords" (Ezekiel 38:4).

God is going to lead Russia and her allies into Israel for the slaughter. He declared, "And it will come to pass at the same time, when Gog comes against the land of Israel, says the Lord GOD, that My fury will show in My face" (Ezekiel 38:18). God then describes the destruction that will fall upon this invading Russian army.

In chapter 39, God gives us the details of the overwhelming defeat. He will leave but a sixth of the invading Russian army—five-sixths will be destroyed! The Israelis will spend seven years burning the implements of war.

God declared, "When I have brought them back from the peoples and gathered them out of their enemies' lands, and I am hallowed in them in the sight of many nations, then they shall know that I am the LORD their God, who sent them into captivity among the nations, but also brought them back to their land, and left none of them captive any longer. And I will not hide My face from them anymore; for I shall have poured out My Spirit on the house of Israel,' says the Lord GOD" (Ezekiel 39:27–29). Notice the three important declarations here. At this time the Jews (Israel) would know that the Lord is God; God's face would no longer be hidden from them; and the Holy Spirit would be poured out on the house of Israel.

This is a significant moment. We are told that God will again pour out His Spirit on the nation of Israel in the day He destroys the Russian army. Earlier in his prophecy, Ezekiel saw the glory of God depart from the temple in Jerusalem (Ezekiel 10:18–19). Jesus prophesied in Matthew 23:38 that their house would be left desolate or deprived of God's presence. When God again pours out His Spirit upon the nation of Israel, His great time clock will be started once again. The world will then begin the last seven-year period.

The Russian invasion of Israel plays a key part in the total plan of God. This military invasion will actually trigger the beginning of the end. Once this last seven-year period is finished, Jesus Christ will come again in glory and will be anointed as King of Kings and Lord of Lords. Then God will establish His everlasting kingdom upon the earth.

It is my very strong conviction that before God's Spirit is placed upon Israel, the church will be taken out of the earth (see Act II). The Bible says, "For I do not desire, brethren, that you should be ignorant of this mystery, lest you should be wise in your own opinion, that blindness in part has happened to Israel until the fullness of the Gentiles has come in" (Romans 11:25). When God no longer blinds the nation of Israel, but has poured His Spirit upon His people, the church will be precluded from being here. Today the Spirit of God has been moving upon the Gentile world, drawing out a bride for Jesus Christ. But when that body of believers is completed, when the fullness of Gentiles has come in, then God's Spirit will deal with the nation Israel. God will take them back and acknowledge them as His people once again. The decisive defeat of the Russian army will give the European nations the opportunity to rise to immediate power. This confederacy will then be the unchallenged major power on the European continent. The Russian invasion of Israel appears to be the next major event on the prophetic horizon.

## THE EUROPEAN UNION

As we look to current events, we see the formation of the European Economic Community, originally known as the Common Market and now referred to as the European Union (EU). The original idea for the formation of the EU came from a group of intellectuals known as the Club of Rome, which formed in 1968. According to its own web site, The Club of Rome is "a global think tank and centre of innovation and initiative . . . (which) brings together scientists, economists, businessmen, international high civil servants, heads of state and former heads of state from all five continents who are convinced that *the future of humankind is not determined once and for all* (emphasis added) and that each human being can contribute to the improvement of our societies."

The confederacy of European nations is relevant to this discussion because each nation in the EU was once a part of the old Roman Empire. This could be coincidence, but it does fit the Scripture without straining the text.

What exactly is the European Union? It's a unique treaty-based institutional framework that defines and manages the economic and political cooperation among its fifteen European member countries. The Union is the latest stage in the process of integration that began in the 1950s by six countries — Belgium, France, Germany, Italy, Luxembourg, and the Netherlands, whose leaders signed the original treaties establishing various forms of European integration. These six countries set up the European Coal and Steel Community (ECSC) High Authority to which the member governments transferred portions of their sovereign powers. Coal and steel were the first things they unified together and after just five years of trading, the value of those commodities increased by 129%. Encouraged by this success, the six nations then pursued the joining together of their military and political fields. However, when those efforts derailed and they decided to focus on unifying the economic front, they became known as the European Economic Community.

In 1955, the EEC signed a treaty in Mesina, Italy, agreeing to merge the separate national markets into a single market that would ensure the free movement of goods, people, capital and services with a wide range of common economic policies. The European Atomic Energy Community was then formed to further the use of nuclear energy for peaceful purposes. This treaty — often referred to as The Treaty of Rome — was signed March 25, 1957 in Rome and came into full force in January, 1958.

Since that time, four enlargements have taken place. Denmark, Ireland and the United Kingdom joined the original six European Community members in 1973. Greece then joined in 1981. At that point, when Greece became the tenth nation of the European Economic Community, I became very excited because I thought, "Wow, ten nations federated together . . . the iron and clay of Daniel's prophecy!" It looked very much like the fulfillment of Nebuchadnezzar's dream. But then in 1986, Spain and Portugal joined and I thought, "Oh, no. They can't join — that makes twelve!" Then Austria, Finland, Sweden joined on January 1, 1995. And more recently, ten nations are being added with another ten seeking to follow. So, thirty-five nations have federated together, forming the largest economic bloc in the world.

For those of us watching these events and comparing them to Daniel's vision, one serious obstacle stood in the way: Russia. As long as Russia existed as a major military threat to the European continent, Western Europe could never rise as a world-dominating power. The Russians had built a tremendous military arsenal and positioned much of their might against Western Europe. As long as Russia possessed such tremendous military capabilities, their power hindered Western Europe or the EU. Even though the nations of the EU have a greater potential gross national product than the United States, and could conceivably become the greatest economic power in the world, they could never rise to world-governing stature as long as Russia overshadowed them.

This barrier has fallen. Events that began to take shape in 1990 startled the whole Western world. The apparent collapse of Communism, the dismantling of the Berlin Wall, the reunification of Germany, and the liberalizing of Eastern Europe sent shockwaves around the world. With the collapse of the Soviet economy, it would appear that God is removing this last obstacle.

On December 31, 1992, the economic borders between the nations of the European Community were removed and a common passport was issued. This was the official realization of the dream of the Club of Rome.

In January of 1999, when the EEC first issued the Euro, the exchange rate between European currency and the U.S. dollar has fluctuated from a low of 0.827 Euros per dollar, to its current rate of 1.356 Euros per dollar. Despite the expected fluctuations, the rise in Euro value is steady and observable. The U.S. dollar has long been the world's standard for monetary purposes, but that is changing. The dollar is declining against the Euro, and it is believed that within five years, the Euro will actually replace the U.S. dollar as the standard world currency.

In analyzing this federation of nations, we can see that it does meet the requirement of Daniel's prophecy in that it is part iron (strong), and yet part clay. Iron and clay can never mix into one homogenous substance. In the same way, this federation of nations can appear unified at times, but it can never be completely unified. Each nation's allegiance to the federation stretches only to the point at which the coalition stops benefiting its own country.

One recent development that has excited me tremendously is that the European Union is now planning to divide Europe into ten sections — five in the west, five in the east. When I heard this, I thought, "All right. Now we're getting back to Daniel's prophecy." This new development has the potential to fulfill the prophecy of the feet with the ten toes.

Since the time of the Roman Empire, there has not been a world-governing nation or empire. Many nations have risen to power, and some have displayed an ambition for world dominance. That was Hitler's ambition. But no nation has yet been able to achieve or attain world dominance. However, the workings among the European Union has all the earmarks of a world-dominating empire. It has all the markings of a pair of ten-toed, iron and clay feet. I am convinced that as we watch the rise of the European Union, we're watching the fulfillment of Nebuchadnezzar's dream.

## SCENE 2: The Antichrist

SCRIPTURE SOMETIMES CALLS HIM "THE BEAST." At other times, it refers to him as "the man of sin," or "the son of perdition." But his most common name is "the Antichrist." The "horn" who will arise to power from the confederacy of ten nations is known by many titles, but one thing is sure: he will be in league with the Devil and do his bidding more than any other man in history. In the days just prior to the second coming of Jesus Christ, he will oppose all that is in heaven and will seek to exalt himself even above God (2 Thessalonians 2:3, 4).

You would think that someone that evil would have trouble finding acceptance in this world. But the fact is, the world is readying itself for his deception — and nowhere is this more evident than in Israel.

Over the years, I've had conversations with Jewish friends about the Messiah. I once asked one particular friend, "How is it that you cannot see that Jesus was the Messiah?" His answer was, "Jesus claimed to be the Son of God, but we believe the Messiah will be a man." They're basing this expectation on a verse in Deuteronomy 18:15, where Moses said, "The LORD your God will raise up for you a Prophet like me from your midst, from your brethren. Him you shall hear."

I pointed out Isaiah 9:6 to him. "For unto us a Child is born, unto us a Son is given; and the government will be upon His shoulder. And His name will be called Wonderful, Counselor, Mighty God, Everlasting Father, Prince of Peace." Jews recognize that this is a Messianic prophecy, yet they still refuse to accept Jesus' claim that He is the Son of God.

As our conversation continued, I asked, "Then you believe the Messiah is yet to come?" And he said, "Yes."

I then asked, "Well, if He's to be a man like you, how will you know when He has come?" My friend responded, "He will lead us in the rebuilding of our temple."

There's the open door. There's the place where the Antichrist can slip in and gain not only acceptance, but also approval. The Bible tells us that the Antichrist will make a covenant with the nation of Israel. But three-and-a-half years into this covenant, he's going to stand in the temple and declare that he is God (Daniel 12:11).

Jesus said, "I have come in My Father's name, and you do not receive Me; if another comes in his own name, him you will receive" (John 5:43). As we can see, Israel is primed and ready to receive the Antichrist as their Messiah because he will allow them and aid them in the rebuilding of the temple.

As prophesied in Revelation 13:4, 16-17, the Antichrist will first come to public prominence with a successful peace program and an entirely new commercial system. He will work wonders with the world economy and will be known for performing miraculous signs. People will stand in awe of him and hail him as the savior of the world. At a time when the world hungers for security, he will satisfy that desire. We already see the powerful peace movements that have risen among the nations of Europe. A growing cry for peace can be heard all over the world; the stage is surely set for the emergence and acceptance of this scripturally predicted man of sin with his plan for universal peace.

The Antichrist will appear to possess miraculous power, but the true source of his strength is Satan. If you recall in Luke chapter 4, Satan tried to tempt Jesus to worship him. Gesturing to the world, Satan said, "All this authority I will give You, and their glory; for this has been delivered to me, and I give it to whomever I wish. Therefore, if You will worship before me, all will be Yours" (4:5-6).

In the King James Version, the verse is translated, "All this power will I give thee, and the glory of them: for that is delivered unto me; and to whomsoever I will I give it." Jesus responded, as we know, by telling Satan, "It is written, 'You shall worship the LORD your God, and Him only you shall serve'" (Luke 4:8). Satan's offer was rejected by Jesus, but it will be accepted by the Antichrist. And Satan will indeed make good on his offer — he will give power, authority, and a throne to the one who will worship him.

As evidence of this "miraculous" power, we're told in Revelation 13:12 that the Antichrist will suffer a deadly wound — perhaps an assassination attempt — but will recover. "And he exercises all the authority of the first beast in his presence, and causes the earth and those who dwell in it to worship the first beast, whose deadly wound was healed." Note the phrase "deadly wound." The implication is that he will die, but will then be "healed." Zechariah describes some of the injuries that will result from this attempt: "A sword shall be against his arm and against his right eye; his arm shall completely wither, and his right eye shall be totally blinded" (Zechariah 11:17).

Note, too, that the assassination attempt and the Antichrist's "miraculous" recovery will cause "the earth and those who dwell in it" to worship him. He will appear to be invincible. It may seem unbelievable that people would ever be so foolish as to actually worship Satan, but we must remember that even today, without miraculous signs to persuade them, there are groups who choose to worship Satan.

Daniel tells us more about the Antichrist. In chapter 11 verse 38 we're told that he "honors a god of fortresses," which is widely interpreted as meaning that instead of worshiping any sort of deity, he will worship military might. And in chapter 7 we are told that he makes war against the saints and overcomes them. The saints in this case are not the church because the gates of hell cannot prevail against the church (Matthew 16:18). Those that are on the earth at that time will worship him but we are told of the horrible fate of those who do so. Revelation 14 warns that whoever worships the beast and takes his mark will "drink of the wine of the wrath of God, which is poured out full strength into the cup of His indignation. He shall be tormented with fire and brimstone in the presence of the holy angels and in the presence of the Lamb. And the smoke of their torment ascends forever and ever; and they have no rest day or night, who worship the beast and his image, and whoever receives the mark of his name" (14:10-11).

Revelation 13:5-6 describes him as being "given a mouth speaking great things and blasphemies." He will have the ability to mesmerize people with his oratory skill. Hitler also possessed that power. As Hitler spoke to the Germans, it was as if they were hypnotized by his speeches. The Antichrist will have that same ability, but in his speeches he will speak blasphemous things against God.

And then, midway through the seven-year period, the Antichrist will do something that will mark the beginning of the countdown of the last 1,290 days before the Lord of glory comes to establish His eternal kingdom.

## THE ABOMINATION OF DESOLATION

Jesus referred to this event as "the abomination of desolation" (Matthew 24:15). This same event is further described in Daniel 9. There we read that while Daniel was in prayer, the angel Gabriel appeared to him.

He said to Daniel, "I have now come forth to give you skill to understand. At the beginning of your supplications the command went out, and I have come to tell you, for you are greatly beloved; therefore consider the matter, and understand the vision:

"Seventy weeks are determined for your people and for your holy city, to finish the transgression, to make an end of sins, to make reconciliation for iniquity, to bring in everlasting righteousness, to seal up vision and prophecy, and to anoint the Most Holy" (Daniel 9:22–24).

The word "week," which in Hebrew is *shabua,* means seven and refers to a week of years, or seven years.

Several events are spoken of here. "To finish the transgression . . . to make an end of sins . . . to make reconciliation for iniquity" — these all belong in one category: they were fulfilled in the first coming of Jesus Christ. "To bring in everlasting righteousness . . . to seal up vision and prophecy . . . to anoint the Most Holy" have not yet been fulfilled, and will not be fulfilled until Jesus comes again.

Gabriel continued, "Know therefore and understand, that from the going forth of the command to restore and build Jerusalem until Messiah the Prince, there shall be seven weeks and sixty-two weeks; the street shall be built again, and the wall, even in troublesome times. And after the sixty-two weeks Messiah shall be cut off, but not for Himself" (Daniel 9:25–26). This is an amazing prophecy. The Jews had been waiting centuries for their Messiah, and here God told Daniel the very day of His arrival.

According to the prophecy, the Messiah was to come sixty-nine times seven (or 483) years after the command went forth to restore and rebuild Jerusalem. Because Daniel used the Babylonian calendar, which contained 360 days to the year, we must multiply 69 x 7 x 360 which equals 173,880 days. On March 14, 445 BC, King Artaxerxes gave the command to Nehemiah to restore and rebuild Jerusalem (2 Chronicles 36:22–23). Exactly 173,880 days later, on AD April 6, 32, Jesus made His triumphant entry into Jerusalem riding on a donkey as prophesied by Zechariah 9:9: "Rejoice greatly, O daughter of Zion! Shout, O daughter of Jerusalem! Behold, your King is coming to you; He is just and having salvation, lowly and riding on a donkey, a colt, the foal of a donkey."

Thus, amid the shouts of His disciples, Jesus made His triumphant entry. They were actually quoting Psalm 118, a messianic Psalm. The section they quoted (verses 24–26) begins with the declaration, "This is the day the LORD has made; we will rejoice and be glad in it." On that same day, as Jesus cried over Jerusalem, He said, "If you had known, even you, especially in this your day, the things that make for your peace! But now they are hidden from your eyes" (Luke 19:42). This was the day the Messiah would come. God kept His promise. However, the Holy Spirit had predicted through Isaiah that He would be despised and rejected by men (Isaiah 53:3) and as the angel said to Daniel, "the Messiah shall be cut off." In perfect fulfillment of these prophecies, Jesus was rejected, crucified, and cut off without receiving the kingdom.

The sixty-nine "sevens" have thus been accounted for, but the angel said seventy sevens had been determined upon the nation Israel. The seventieth "week" of Daniel has not yet been fulfilled. The end of the seventieth seven will bring the completion of all the visions and prophecies, the most Holy place will be anointed, and Jesus will establish God's eternal, righteous Kingdom.

Jesus Christ was cut off without receiving His kingdom. He did not bring in the age of everlasting righteousness, as is so evident today as we look around and see the world in which we live. The most Holy has not yet been anointed. Therefore, all the prophecies in Daniel have not yet been fulfilled. We have yet to complete the seventieth seven-year period.

The angel continued to tell Daniel, "Then he [the prince who is to come] shall confirm a covenant with many for one week." In the midst of the week, or final seven-year period, he will break the covenant and set up the abomination which causes the desolation (Daniel 9:27).

When the disciples asked Jesus what the signs of the end of the world would be, He replied, "Therefore when you see the 'abomination of desolation,' spoken of by Daniel the prophet, standing in the holy place" (whoever reads, let him understand), "then let those who are in Judea flee to the mountains. Let him who is on the housetop not go down to take anything out of his house. And let him who is in the field not go back to get his clothes" (Matthew 24:15–18). The fact that Jesus referred to this event as future in His day and related it to the time of His second coming precludes any interpretation that would place the seventieth seven in past history.

What is the "abomination of desolation" that Daniel the prophet spoke about? The Antichrist will make a covenant with the nation Israel. As part of that covenant, he will grant the Israelites the right to rebuild the temple in Jerusalem and will promise to bring them peace.

Then, after three-and-a-half years, the Antichrist will violate this agreement and cause the daily sacrifices and offerings to cease. He will stand in the holy place of the rebuilt temple, declare that he is God, and demand to be worshiped (2 Thessalonians 2:4). This is the abomination (a horribly disgusting act) that causes the desolation (wretchedness; devastation) of the holy place. The word desolation also means "great agony or emptiness," and is used to refer to the great tribulation. This one act will open the eyes of the Jews, who will finally see that they have been deceived by the Antichrist. Many will then flee to sanctuary in southern Jordan.

## THE ANTICHRIST AND ISRAEL

A few years ago when we were in Israel, we saw bumper stickers, placards, and signs throughout the land proclaiming, "The Messiah is coming." Israel is watching and waiting. Many Jews today have come to the conclusion that the only hope that they have for their survival is the coming of the Messiah. The problem is, the true Messiah has already come and has already been rejected by His own.

The Antichrist will be revealed to those who shall perish, because they did not receive the love of the truth that they might be saved. He cannot be revealed until he who hinders is taken out of the way. The hindering force that is keeping the Antichrist from being revealed today is the power of the Holy Spirit working within the church. Notice the Antichrist will come to those who are unrighteous, those who are to perish because they would not receive the truth. Nowhere in the Scriptures is there any mention of the church being on the earth during the reign of the Antichrist. It is clear then that only after Jesus Christ takes His church away will the man of sin be revealed. The Antichrist will then be free to establish a covenant with Israel and promise to help them rebuild their temple.

As mentioned earlier, many Jews feel that the Messiah will be a man just as Moses was, and they believe they will recognize the Messiah when one comes along who will help them rebuild their temple. Many of the rabbis are expecting the Messiah to come soon. In light of the fact that Daniel speaks of the covenant that the Antichrist will make with Israel, and the prophecy of Jesus in John 5:43 when He told the Jews, "I have come in My Father's name, and you do not receive Me; if another comes in his own name, him you will receive," it is easy to see just how ready so many are to accept the false Messiah.

## THE ANTICHRIST AND THE TEMPLE

It is fascinating to see the great desire of many Jews today to rebuild the temple. Dr. Assur Koffman, a professor at the Hebrew University in Jerusalem, is a part of this movement. He has been engaged in extensive research to locate the possible site of Solomon's Temple, and has concluded that it stood some 322 feet north of the Dome of the Rock. According to his investigation, the Holy of Holies stood over what is known today as the Dome of the Spirits, or the Dome of the Tablets. If his conclusions are correct, they would be very significant. The rebuilding of the Jewish temple could be accomplished without removing the Dome of the Rock. This would prevent a full scale Jihad (holy war) by the Muslims. This location for the temple would have interesting ramifications in Old Testament interpretation. When Ezekiel had his vision in which he saw the rebuilt temple, he was ordered to measure it. In Ezekiel 42:20, he tells us the temple had a wall around it about five hundred cubits (a cubit is about 1.43 feet) long and five hundred cubits wide, "to make a separation between the sanctuary and the profane place" (KJV).

The Dome of the Rock has approximately seven hundred feet of Arabic writing around the top of it, both inside and out, which seeks to profane Jesus Christ. It declares, "God is not begotten neither does He beget" which is a direct attack against the New Testament truth that "God so loved the world that He gave His only begotten Son" (John 3:16).

71

In Revelation 11, John also had a vision of the new temple that would stand in Jerusalem during the tribulation period. He too was ordered to measure it, but was told not to measure the outer court, as it had been given to the heathen. If the new temple were to be built with the Dome of the Spirits as the site for the Holy of Holies, the Dome of the Rock could stand behind a wall similar to the one Ezekiel measured. It would be located in the area that would have been the outer court of Solomon's Temple. I believe that building a wall just north of the Dome of the Rock, giving the Jews the north side of the Temple Mount as the site for their new temple, will be the solution offered by the Antichrist. This ingenious answer to one of the most difficult political problems ever faced by mankind will cause the Antichrist to be acclaimed by the world as a brilliant peacemaker. The Jews will hail him as the Messiah, leading to the beginning of the final seven-year week described in Daniel's prophecy.

Three-and-a-half years later, he will return to stand in the Holy Place and boast that he is God (Matthew 24:15; 2 Thessalonians 2:3-4). The Jews will then realize their mistake and flee to the wilderness where God has prepared a place to shelter them for the final three-and-a-half years of the Antichrist's tenure. During this same period, the world will go through a time of trouble unparalleled in its history. As Jesus said in Matthew 24:21, the tribulation will be worse than anything the world has ever seen before or will ever see again. These terrifying events are chronicled in detail in Revelation, chapters 6 through 19.

## THE PREPARATION

As we have seen, many of the main props are now in place on the world stage. The actors are taking their places and the final scene is ready to begin. The angel of the Lord told Daniel that seventy sevens are determined upon the nation Israel. Sixty-nine of those sevens have already been fulfilled.

The angel also said that the timespan from the commandment to restore and rebuild Jerusalem to the coming of the Messiah would be exactly 483 years, but the Messiah would be cut off and receive nothing, and the Jews would be dispersed (Daniel 9:24–26). Just as the angel told Daniel, Jesus the Messiah was cut off without receiving His kingdom, and the Jews were dispersed by the Romans in AD 70.

Since the crucifixion, God's prophetic calendar has stood still. One important seven-year period, the seventieth seven of Daniel, is yet to come. This will complete the entire prophecy of Daniel 9.

In His first coming, Jesus Christ accomplished reconciliation with God by dying for our sins. He made an end of our iniquities through His death on the cross. The later portion of that prophecy, which includes bringing in everlasting righteousness and His eternal kingdom, the completion of all prophecies, and the anointing of the most Holy remains yet to be fulfilled. These prophetic elements will come to pass at Christ's second coming. During this last seven-year period, the man of sin, or the Antichrist, will be revealed. Jesus Christ referred to him as "the one who shall come in his own name" and whom the Jews will receive (John 5:43). This man of sin will arise from a confederation of ten European nations. The Antichrist will establish a completely new world order.

## SCENE 3: Signs of the Times

THOUGH WE HAVE NO INDICATION OF whom the Antichrist is at this moment in time, we do know that certain "signs" will begin to point toward the end. When Jesus spoke of the signs which would indicate that His return was near, He described the very events that we see happening today. He told us that when we see these things begin to come to pass we should look up and lift up our heads, for our redemption is getting close. Over and over He warned of the necessity of watching and being ready.

## SIGN: ELECTRONIC FUNDS TRANSFER

We are told in the Scriptures that the Antichrist will cause everyone to receive a number or mark on his right hand or forehead. No one will be able to buy or sell without this number (Revelation 13:17). This may sound impossible, but in the 1970s we began to accustom ourselves to a cashless society. Various banks offered services using little plastic cards which held coded numbers. It was possible to go to the store with a card instead of cash. The clerk processed our transaction and with a simple signature we could obtain almost any item without the exchange of money.

The day is near when money will have absolutely no value in buying or selling. The Antichrist will base his commercial program upon a system that transfers funds with coded identification numbers. All transactions will be processed electronically by computer. Those who are on earth after the rapture of the church will be assigned a number or mark. No one will be able to buy or sell unless they have that mark.

In America, we are well on our way to a cashless society. Over the last thirty years, technological advances have all but eliminated the need to write checks or pay with cash. Many major companies no longer issue payroll checks, but will automatically put funds in your bank account so that you don't need to handle cash. On-line banking enables us to pay bills without writing a check, handling money, or licking a stamp.

Though still in the future, the ability to transfer funds electronically carries the potential to control theft. If no one was able to buy or sell without access to a computerized system, thieves couldn't sell stolen goods without producing an identification number. Stealing money would be useless because cash would be obsolete. Think of all the crime this would eliminate. No more liquor store holdups. No more service station robberies. No more home robberies. It's a perfect solution for today's crime problem.

We're not at that point yet, but we're working our way there. Most people make most of their purchases today with either credit cards or debit cards. It's very easy; very convenient. But there's a problem with the credit/ debit card system. How can the retailer be certain that the person presenting the card is the one entitled to its use?

SIGN: PERSONAL IDENTIFICATION

Most criminals arrested in California carry from five to thirty stolen credit cards. When a thief steals a wallet, he's usually more interested in the credit cards than the money. With a credit card he can rob an entire account or immediately charge merchandise for future resale before the card is reported as stolen.

Researchers are presently working on a foolproof identification system to eliminate the problem of lost or stolen credit cards. One of the suggestions is to use a laser tattoo. A laser beam has been developed that can painlessly brand livestock in one thirty-two thousandth of a second.

Laser beams are also being used for microdata processing. Using this technology, the entire Bible can now be printed on the head of a pin. It would be very easy to write a miniaturized complete personal history so small as to be invisible, and have it placed on a convenient spot on your body (such as your hand) by laser beam. I don't know whether or not a laser tattoo will be the ultimate solution to the credit card system's identification problems, but it does present a very plausible answer. The tattooing would be totally painless and would provide a sure-fire form of identification that no one could duplicate or steal.

One suggestion to this problem came from a firm in Florida called Applied Digital Solutions. They developed a chip about the size of a grain of rice that can be inserted under the skin and scanned like the barcodes on merchandise. At a global security conference this technology was presented as an advance over credit cards and smart cards, which are subject to theft and identity fraud. This chip was declared to be a "loss-proof solution" whose unique, under-the-skin format could be used for a variety of identification applications in the security and financial world.

In October 2004, the Food and Drug Administration gave approval to Applied Digital Solutions, latest offering, the VeriChip TM. According to the company, their plan was to market the chip which would contain personal medical records to hospitals, doctors and patients as a way to better monitor and care for patients.

When the *Washington Post* ran that announcement of the FDA's approval, over 1 million VeriChips TM had already been implanted in animals. The technology enables horse owners to electronically "brand" their horses; biochips containing the identity and addresses of pet owners are regularly inserted in dogs and cats.

More alarming is the fact that at the printing of that article, 7,000 chips had been sold for human use — and 1,000 had already been implanted.[3]

---

[3] Stein, R., October 14, 2004. http://www.washingtonpost.com/wp-dyn/articles/A29954-2004Oct13.html

The Bible states that the man who will arise from a confederation of European nations to rule the world will order everyone to receive a mark either on his right hand or on his forehead, and that no one will be able to buy or sell without this mark. It looks as if we're coming close to this today. Grocery stores already use scanners to log in the UPC codes on the items that you have selected. It would be very simple to hold your hand with its tattooed mark or number under the scanner so that your total grocery bill would be automatically deducted from your computerized bank account. The capacities for such procedures have already been developed and the possibilities of application are endless.

What the Bible predicted nearly two thousand years ago was a scientific fantasy at the time, but it has become a practical reality today with the development of computer technology.

This is just one of the signs. What are some of the other signs we should look for before the Antichrist makes his entrance?

## SIGN: WORLD CRISIS

Sitting on the Mount of Olives one day, the disciples asked Jesus about the end of the age. "Tell us, when will these things be? And what will be the sign when all these things will be fulfilled?" (Mark 13:4). Jesus answered, "Take heed that no one deceives you. For many will come in My name, saying, 'I am He', and will deceive many. But when you hear of wars and rumors of wars, do not be troubled; for such things must happen, but the end is not yet. For nation will rise against nation, and kingdom against kingdom. And there will be earthquakes in various places, and there will be famines and troubles. These are the beginnings of sorrows" (13:5-8).

In Luke's telling of that conversation, he writes that Jesus said, "And there will be great earthquakes in various places, and famines and pestilences; and there will be fearful sights and great signs from heaven" (Luke 21:11). Great earthquakes. Famines. Pestilence. Fearful sights. That sounds like a description of our world today. Large, devastating earthquakes are a regular occurrence around the globe. The 2004 tsunami in Indonesia was the result of an earthquake in the Indian Ocean. Hurricanes are increasing in both frequency and intensity — just think of the havoc Katrina wreaked.

Pestilence — fatal, epidemic disease — is a global problem. Doctors are issuing dire warnings about the Bird Flu, which has the potential to cause a deadly pandemic. Supergerms resist every antibiotic the medical field tries to use against them. AIDS is spreading worldwide.

In fact, the entire African continent is in a social chaos right now because of the AIDS epidemic. The disease has orphaned hundreds of thousands of children, creating a problem we don't know how to begin to tackle. And though AIDS is the leading killer of adults between the ages of 25 and 44, hunger kills more people than AIDS, tuberculosis and malaria combined. Worldwide, 850 million people are chronically hungry, and every five seconds, a child somewhere dies of hunger.[4]

The world wants a solution. As these problems rise, it's interesting to note that when those of us who study biblical prophecy begin talking about the end of the world, we are now being taken seriously. No longer are we classified with religious fanatics. Serious-minded people looking at our world in crisis are beginning to conclude that something must be done. The usual solution provided by the world is simple and direct: leaders say that we can no longer continue as separate nations with separate goals and ideals. We must surrender to a globally-federated body, a one-world government. Along with that, they conclude that we also need a one-world religion. Not long ago, I saw a bumper sticker that read, "God is too big for one religion." Many people are dedicated to working toward these universalistic goals,

---

[4] http://www.guardian.co.uk/slideshow/page/0,,1921631,00.html

which again, is exactly what the Bible says will happen. We're moving toward a one-world government in which one man will arise who will dominate all mankind.

## SIGN: THE EARTH STAGGERS LIKE A DRUNKEN MAN

Global warming is a hot topic these days. You almost can't get through the day without hearing someone talking about fossil fuel emissions and greenhouse gases. The belief is that the burning of fossil fuels, combined with deforestation, is warming the earth to dangerous levels. Fossil fuels emit a concentration of heat-trapping gases. Deforestation removes trees that would otherwise trap carbon and other particles released through pollution. The combination of those two factors has resulted in a change in earth's temperature. While some scientists are reluctant to jump on that bandwagon, a large percentage have concluded that the earth is, indeed, warming up — and dangerously so.

Consider these facts:

- According to data compiled by NOAA and NASA, the US's recognized atmosphere and space experts, the average surface temperature of earth has risen 1.2 to 1.4°F in the last century.

- Historically, the warmest temperatures on record have all occurred within the past 15 years.

- At the current rate, it is estimated that global temperatures will rise another 2.5 to 10.4°F by the end of this century.[5]

In addition to global warming, another ongoing concern is the condition of the ozone layer. The earth is surrounded with a blanket of ozone gas in the stratosphere. This layer of gas plays a very important part in man's survival by acting as a filter and protecting us from bombardment by the sun's lethal ultraviolet rays. In the book of Job, God mentions a "swaddling-band" around the earth (Job 38:9). This may have been a reference to the ozone layer that surrounds our planet. If the ozone layer were brought down to the earth's surface, it would form a blanket only three feet thick.

Scientists have long claimed that we're in danger of destroying this protective layer. The first suggestion of this came back in 1974 when scientists concluded that aerosol products release fluorocarbon gases into the air which cause the ozone to combine with nitrogen gas to form nitric oxide. Supersonic jets that fly fifteen hundred miles an hour at fifty-five thousand feet also pose a threat to the ozone blanket. The gases emitted through the exhausts of these supersonic jets combine

---

[5] http://www.epa.gov/climatechange/basicinfo.html

with oxygen and react with the ozone, diminishing the protective shield against the ultraviolet rays.

The effects of this depleted ozone shield can be felt any time you spend too much time exposed to the sun. Several years ago, I baptized several hundred people in the ocean, and as the result of several hours of exposure in the sun during that service, I received severe burns on my head. My doctor informed me they were ultraviolet burns — burns commonly associated with the depletion of the ozone layer.

In addition to aerosol products and supersonic jets, the releasing of great clouds of gases during the testing of atomic bombs is also detrimental to the existing ozone blanket. If we were to have an atomic war with a number of nuclear devices detonated within the atmosphere, the worst effect wouldn't necessarily be the initial destruction. It could very well be the destruction of the ozone layer. Without this blanket, the ultraviolet rays of the sun would begin to cook people alive.

In Revelation 16 we read that when the fourth vial is poured out by the angel during the great tribulation, power is given unto the sun to scorch men with fire (Revelation 16:8-9). This could very well be a description of ultraviolet radiation effects as the result of the disappearing ozone layer. This calamity was predicted two thousand years ago, before anyone even knew that a protective ozone blanket existed in our atmosphere.

Not only are we destroying the ozone layer and raising the earth's temperature, but man is also guilty of harming our environment by recklessly using chemicals to control pests. We've concluded that the only way to produce enough crops to keep us all from starving to death is through the use of massive amounts of pesticides. But we don't fully know the consequences and side effects of these chemicals on our health, our lives, or our future. Years ago, one of the most prominent insecticides in widespread use was DDT. Over time, we discovered that DDT didn't disintegrate in the soil but remained in its same chemical form — and eventually found its way into rivers and then into oceans, where it destroyed seaweed, microscopic plant and animal life, and fish. DDT was subsequently banned in the United States, but it is still in use in some parts of the world.

The fact that we can destroy a major portion of the life within the ocean also coincides with another plague spoken of in the book of Revelation. John saw a great mountain burning with fire fall into the sea, and a third of the creatures living within the sea were destroyed (Revelation 8:8).

And then there's overpopulation. Experts predict that unless something dramatic is done to curb the spiral of population growth, by the year 2200 the earth will be wall-to-wall with people. The earth's population has already risen to over 6.6 billion people, and continues to grow at the rate of two percent of the total population each year. Even now we cannot feed all the people on the planet. The majority of people on earth today go to bed hungry and undernourished. As the population increases, the demand for food increases, but the supply of food decreases. And so we see food prices rising sky-high.

Jesus said that famine would be one of the signs of the end of the world (Matthew 24:7). Revelation tells of a time that is coming when a measure of wheat (roughly a quart) will be sold for a day's wage (Revelation 6:6). So if you're planning to be around for this coming catastrophe and want to hedge your bets, don't invest your money in silver or gold. Put it in wheat. What good will your gold be if you can't buy anything with it? In fact, James warns of the last days, "Come now, you rich, weep and howl for your miseries that are coming upon you! Your riches are corrupted, and your garments are moth-eaten. Your gold and silver are corroded, and their corrosion will be a witness against you and will eat your flesh like fire. You have heaped up treasure in the last days" (James 5:1-3).

Man has also created a new generation of incredibly devastating weapons. The United States is known to possess nuclear weapons, chemical weapons and biological weapons. In speaking of the end of the world, Jesus said, "Unless those days were shortened, no flesh would be saved" (Matthew 24:22). For centuries the idea that man could completely destroy himself was considered preposterous. But now we have enough explosive power to destroy every man, woman and child living on the planet. Our military leaders warn us that a major nuclear war could easily mean the end of the world.

It's clear that our energy resources are being deleted at a rapid rate. We used to take oil out of the ground as if there were no tomorrow. We thought we certainly had enough energy reserves to last for the foreseeable future. Now we are constantly being asked to curb our normal use of energy until science can discover some alternate resource. Our fossil-fuel reserves are limited, and scientists predict the approaching end for this type of energy.

As mentioned in the previous section, earthquakes are increasing in frequency and intensity around the world. This is another striking sign that Jesus said would signal the time of His return (Matthew 24:7).

Physicists are also getting into the act of prophesying doom. In studying the earth's structure, they find that the ions affected by the earth's magnetism are lined up differently from what is now true north. Some scientists believe this is the result of a polar axis shift. According to some researchers, these shifts occur approximately every five thousand years. It has been speculated that the last polar axis shift coincided with the flood of Noah's time. This could well mean that we're overdue for another major shift. Some scientists believe that during a polar axis shift, islands disappear, mountains melt into valleys, and ocean floors become land masses. The whole area of Utah used to be a vast ocean. You can find ocean shell fossils at seven thousand feet above sea level on the south rim of the Grand Canyon, indicating a major change in the oceans and the mountain structures from the past. Such changes supposedly happened during the last polar axis shift. It is impossible to calculate the geological damage that will result from such an upheaval of nature.

When we read passages that describe an event where "every mountain and island was moved out of its place" (Revelation 6:14), and "The earth shall stagger like a drunken man, and shall sway to and fro like a hammock" (Isaiah 24:20 ASV), it's easy to wonder if God is possibly foretelling a polar axis shift.

## SIGN: CREATION AND TERMINATION

It used to be considered scientifically naive to talk about a specific time of creation, but physicists are now realizing that there must have been such a day. Sir James Jeans in his book *The Universe Around Us* says that the universe is like a giant clock that was wound up and is slowly running down. A prime example of the evidence that points to a specific starting point in time for our universe is found in our own sun. In order to give off the vast amount of energy that allows for our survival on planet earth, the sun must consume over two million tons of its own mass every second. This creates a huge problem if, as evolutionists claim, the universe has existed for billions of years. Over an infinite stretch of time, not only our sun but also every star in the entire universe would have burned out its fuel supply billions of years ago. A star with enough mass to burn literally forever would have to be as large as the universe itself. Therefore, it is now commonly acceptable to look back to a specific point in time called the day of creation. However, scientists are now looking to the future at a much more disturbing point of time called "the day of termination."

## SIGN: SOCIAL CHAOS

Social scientists are not concerned as much with the physical aspects of the planet as with the behavior of the men upon it. Even if we manage to avoid a terminal, physical catastrophe, many experts are so alarmed at the rising increase in social hostility that they question the probability of human survival.

Social behavior is so bad that police departments and law enforcement agencies are unable to cope with the number of crimes they're expected to handle. Have you called a policeman lately? If you are the victim of a crime, the police will come out and make a report, but they offer very little encouragement about the possibility of you recovering any of your possessions. If a child has run away, they will file a missing person's report. But there's very little promise of a happy ending to the crisis. So much crime exists that many experts have actually given up any hope of re-establishing law and order.

Paul wrote to Timothy, "But know this, that in the last days perilous times will come: For men will be lovers of themselves, lovers of money, boasters, proud, blasphemers, disobedient to parents, unthankful, unholy, unloving, unforgiving, slanderers, without self-control, brutal, despisers of good, traitors, headstrong, haughty, lovers of pleasure rather than lovers of God" (2 Timothy 3:1–4). Sadly, the Bible describes men as we see them today.

How ironic that with all the scientists, the professors, the militarists, and the sociologists crying, "The end of the world!" The church has been silent. It may be that the church is so preoccupied with its dwindling attendance rolls and increased financial burdens that it hasn't noticed the signs of the times.

## A CONCLUSIVE END

When Christians speak of the world and its end, we mean something entirely different than the scientists. The secular expert is talking about the end of the world in a physical sense. But when Christians talk about the end of the world, we are speaking of the destruction of a set and ordered system that rejects God. The world order around us that is governed by Satan in rebellion against God is coming to a final and conclusive end. We, the church, are waiting for a new form of government: a monarchy that will embrace the entire world and endure forever. We're waiting for the kingdom of God to come when righteousness will cover the earth as the waters cover the sea.

Man has tried just about every conceivable form of government. City-states, monarchies, democracies, dictatorships, and various forms of socialism have all been tried with varying degrees of success and failure. Man has attempted many different ways to govern himself, but every form of government has ultimately deteriorated. No matter how theoretically perfect the system might appear to be, man cannot rule himself without greed and corruption setting in. Most forms of government have been able to endure for only about two hundred years before totally disintegrating.

There seems to be no way out of the economic, social, or universal problems confronting us today. As we look at the nations, there is no dominant power in the world today. The world is divided and the nations are in perplexity. Even the experts don't know what to do about the economic situation, the energy crisis, or increasing food shortages. Just as Scripture said would happen during the end times, the nations are perplexed (Luke 21:25).

Amidst all this chaos and disorder, men are looking for a leader. And that leader is coming. He's going to come in his own name, proclaiming marvelous things, and men will be drawn after him. He's going to have an incredibly efficient and universal economic program of computerized commerce, and will appear to offer the peace for which the world so desperately longs.

Is it all just a coincidence? Or did God know what He was talking about when He spoke of these things two thousand years ago? Jesus said, "Now when these things begin to happen, look up and lift up your heads, because your redemption draws near" (Luke 21:28). The church ought to be expectantly looking up. And we should find our voice. Instead of standing silently by, we should be proclaiming, "The end of the world!"

## NOT GLOOM, BUT BLOOM

This is not a cry of despair or of doom and gloom, for the end of this world system will mean an end of greed and hatred, wars and famines, sickness and death. The commercial exploitation of others, creating untold personal misery, will be gone forever.

The prophet Isaiah called, "Ho! Everyone who thirsts, come to the waters; and you who have no money, come, buy and eat. Yes, come, buy wine and milk without money and without price" (Isaiah 55:2). The end of this world system will mark an end of the world governed by man in rebellion against God, and the beginning of a new world governed by God and marked by peace like a river (Isaiah 66:12). It marks the beginning of a world where there is no pain or sorrow, for "God will wipe away every tear" (Revelation 21:4). Isaiah tells us that "the eyes of the blind shall be opened, and the ears of the deaf shall be unstopped. . . the lame shall leap like a deer, and the tongue of the dumb sing" (Isaiah 35:5-6). He also tells us, in Isaiah 2:4, that men will "beat their swords into plowshares, and their spears into pruning hooks." In other words, military budgets will be diverted to agricultural development. Last year, the nations of the world spent over one trillion dollars in military expenditures. If this amount of money had been spent for agricultural development, not one person would have starved to death.

The prophet Micah tells us, "Nation shall not lift up sword against nation, neither shall they learn war anymore, but everyone shall sit under his vine and under his fig tree, and no one shall make them afraid" (Micah 4:3–4). That does not sound like doom and gloom to me, but like a beautiful ideal world where I desire to live. I long for this new world and pray daily, "Thy Kingdom come, Thy will be done in earth, even as it is in heaven." The waiting is difficult. "Even so, come quickly, Lord Jesus" (Revelation 22:20).

## THINGS TO COME

Our world is in a death-dive. We've peaked, and now we're plunging rapidly to the end. Moral rot and decay have so corrupted the planks of our society that they will soon crumble and fall. The only hope for escape is for Jesus Christ to snatch His followers out of this mad, fatal plunge.

In the unfolding drama of the end times, it's time to turn to Act II: the rapture.

## ABNORMAL SEXUAL ACTIVITY

- Romans 1:17-32
- 2 Peter 2:10, 14; 3:3
- Jude 18

## BLASPHEMY

- 2 Timothy 3:2
- 2 Peter 2:3, 3:3
- Jude 18

## CHRISTIAN FAITH DEPARTURE

- 2 Thessalonians 2:3
- 1 Timothy 4:1, 3-4
- 2 Timothy 3:5; 4:3-4
- 2 Peter 3:3-4

## CONSCIENCE SEARING

- 1 Timothy 4:2

## DEMONIC ACTIVITY

- Genesis 6:1-4
- 1 Timothy 4:1-3

## FALSE PEACE

- 1 Thessalonians 5:1-3

## FALSE PROPHETS AND ANTICHRISTS

- Matthew 24:5, 11
- 2 Peter 2:1-2

## INCREASE IN SPEED AND KNOWLEDGE

- Daniel 12:4

## LAWLESSNESS

- Psalm 78:8
- Proverbs 30:14-19
- 2 Timothy 3:2-3

## LOVERS OF PLEASURE

- 2 Timothy 3:2, 4

## MATERIALISM

- 2 Timothy 3:1-2

## POLITICS AND RELIGIONS IN ISRAEL

- Matthew 24:32-34

## REJECTION OF GOD AND GOD'S WORD

- Psalm 2:1-3
- 2 Timothy 4:3-4; 2
- 2 Peter 3:3-4, 16

## VIOLENCE

- Genesis 6:11, 13
- Revelation 9:21

## WARS AND RUMORS OF WARS

- Joel 3:9-10
- Matthew 24:6-7

Act II

# THE
# RAPTURE

## The Plot Thickens

IN ACT I, WE CAUGHT our first glimpse of the world stage in the last days. We met the main characters in our drama: the nation of Israel, the Antichrist, and Jesus Christ. That first Act described a world wracked by devastation; a world hungering for change. With those first scenes behind us and the tension mounting, the curtain draws back to reveal Act II — the depiction of a supernatural occurrence; a glorious event for the church of Jesus Christ.

The Bible tells us that our King will return one day *with* His church — but before He arrives *with* His church, He's coming *for* His church. It's important that we keep these two events separate — that we distinguish between His coming *for* His church in the rapture, and His coming *with* His church in the second coming.

When Paul came to Thessalonica, the Jews stirred up so much trouble within the city that he couldn't stay long and had to leave abruptly. Many people had received Jesus Christ through Paul's ministry and Paul shared with them the glorious kingdom of God that Jesus was going to establish upon the earth.

Some of the believers in the church had died. And the Thessalonian believers — not fully understanding the teaching of the kingdom of God — were sorrowing over the fact that these friends had died before the Lord returned to establish the kingdom. So Paul wrote his letter to encourage and comfort the church in Thessalonica and to correct their mistaken notions about some key issues they held.

One of the main notions Paul had to correct was their view on Christ's coming. The Thessalonians wrongly believed that since their friends had died before the Lord's return, their friends would miss out on the kingdom of God. Essentially, they thought, "Poor Joe, he died before the Lord came back, so now he's missing out."

But Paul corrected that belief when he wrote,

BUT I DO NOT WANT YOU TO BE IGNORANT, BRETHREN, CONCERNING THOSE WHO HAVE FALLEN ASLEEP, LEST YOU SORROW AS OTHERS WHO HAVE NO HOPE. FOR IF WE BELIEVE THAT JESUS DIED AND ROSE AGAIN, EVEN SO GOD WILL BRING WITH HIM THOSE WHO SLEEP IN JESUS. FOR THIS WE SAY TO YOU BY THE WORD OF THE LORD, THAT WE WHO ARE ALIVE AND REMAIN UNTIL THE COMING OF THE LORD WILL BY NO MEANS PRECEDE THOSE WHO ARE ASLEEP (1 THESSALONIANS 4:13-15).

## SCENE 1: Caught Up

In 1 Corinthians 15:51-52 Paul said, "Behold, I tell you a mystery: We shall not all sleep, but we shall all be changed — in a moment, in the twinkling of an eye, at the last trumpet. For the trumpet will sound, and the dead will be raised incorruptible, and we shall be changed." You won't even realize it's happened until it's all over. Suddenly, you're in the presence of the Lord with all the church!

We, the church, will be changed. Paul wrote to the Philippians, "For our citizenship is in heaven, from which we also eagerly wait for the Savior, the Lord Jesus Christ, who will transform our lowly body that it may be conformed to His glorious body, according to the working by which He is able even to subdue all things to Himself" (Philippians 3:20-21). Describing this metamorphosis Paul wrote to the Corinthinians, "For this corruptible must put on incorruption, and this mortal must put on immortality" (1 Corinthians 15:53). At the second coming we will then return with Jesus Christ. Jude 14 tells us, "Behold, the Lord comes with ten thousands of His saints." Further, in 1 Thessalonians Paul writes,

> FOR THE LORD HIMSELF WILL DESCEND FROM
> HEAVEN WITH A SHOUT, WITH THE VOICE OF
> AN ARCHANGEL, AND WITH THE TRUMPET OF
> GOD. AND THE DEAD IN CHRIST WILL RISE
> FIRST. THEN WE WHO ARE ALIVE AND REMAIN
> SHALL BE CAUGHT UP TOGETHER WITH THEM
> IN THE CLOUDS TO MEET THE LORD IN THE AIR
> (4:16-17).

The term "rapture" refers to that moment when Jesus Christ snatches His church out of this world. Scripture tells us it shall happen suddenly and without any notice. It's important to note again that the rapture of the church and the second coming of Jesus Christ are completely different events. At the rapture, Jesus is coming for His saints.

Some people argue that the word "rapture" isn't in the Bible, and thus, they don't believe in the rapture of the church. But it all depends on your understanding of the language.

In the Greek, the word translated "caught up" is *harpazo*, meaning "to be snatched away with force." In the Latin Vulgate translation, the word is *rapare* or *raptus*, and from that word *rapare* we get our word "rapture." It is the same Greek word, *harpazo* which is "caught up" or "snatched away" in English. Note, it is the same word, just different language translations. So, when you read "caught up" in English, you are reading "rapture" in Latin.

## THE SEQUENCE

What we learn from the Bible concerning the rapture of the church is that those believers who have already died will be coming with Jesus when He comes for the rest of us. Those here on the earth will not precede those who have died. The Lord will then descend with a shout and the voice of the archangel and the trump of God. The Lord is not coming to the earth at this time (His second coming), but we who are alive and remain will be "caught up" (raptured) to meet the Lord in the air, with those believers who have already died before us.

Several Scriptures teach us about the rapture. In John 14:1-3, Jesus told His disciples,

> LET NOT YOUR HEART BE TROUBLED; YOU BELIEVE IN GOD, BELIEVE ALSO IN ME. IN MY FATHER'S HOUSE ARE MANY MANSIONS; IF IT WERE NOT SO, I WOULD HAVE TOLD YOU. I GO TO PREPARE A PLACE FOR YOU. AND IF I GO AND PREPARE A PLACE FOR YOU, I WILL COME AGAIN AND RECEIVE YOU TO MYSELF; THAT WHERE I AM, THERE YOU MAY BE ALSO.

Jesus promised that He would come and receive us unto Himself; that where He is, there we will be also. Likewise, in 1 Corinthians chapter 15 beginning with verse 51, Paul says,

> BEHOLD, I TELL YOU A MYSTERY: WE SHALL NOT ALL SLEEP, BUT WE SHALL ALL BE CHANGED — IN A MOMENT, IN THE TWINKLING OF AN EYE, AT THE LAST TRUMPET. FOR THE TRUMPET WILL SOUND, AND THE DEAD WILL BE RAISED INCORRUPTIBLE, AND WE SHALL BE CHANGED. FOR THIS CORRUPTIBLE MUST PUT ON INCORRUPTION, AND THIS MORTAL MUST PUT ON IMMORTALITY. SO WHEN THIS CORRUPTIBLE HAS PUT ON INCORRUPTION, AND

THIS MORTAL HAS PUT ON IMMORTALITY, THEN SHALL BE BROUGHT TO PASS THE SAYING THAT IS WRITTEN: DEATH IS SWALLOWED UP IN VICTORY, O DEATH, WHERE IS YOUR STING? O HADES, WHERE IS YOUR VICTORY?

What does this tell us about the rapture? It tells us that it will occur at the last trump, and that it's going to take place very quickly, in a twinkling of an eye.

## THE TRUMP OF GOD VS. 7TH TRUMPET OF ANGEL

Now this "trump" is not to be confused with the seventh trumpet in the book of Revelation. The seventh trumpet, mentioned in Revelation 11:15, follows the great tribulation period. But the trumpet referred to in 1 Thessalonians 4:16 will sound when the church is raptured.

The seventh trumpet in the book of Revelation is declared to be a woe. When the fourth trumpet has sounded, the angel said, "Woe, woe, woe" to the inhabitants of the earth by reason of the three trumpets that are yet to sound. When the fifth trumpet sounds, again it declares that one woe is past, and two woes are yet to come. When the sixth trumpet sounds, it's declared, "The second woe is past, and the third woe is coming quickly" (Revelation 11:14).

So the seventh trumpet is a trumpet of woe, rather than a trumpet of hallelujah or praise to God.

## METAMORPHOSIS

What we learn from this passage of Scripture is that when the rapture happens, we will go through a metamorphosis. Our bodies will be changed in a mere moment, in a twinkling of an eye. At that point, we will be given our new incorruptible bodies.

Our parents and their genealogies gave us these earthly bodies. Sometimes you can tell just by looking at a person that they are related to their parents, but even when the similarity is not noticeable, the genetic structure of the body can be traced directly to our parental lineage. However, through the centuries, a breakdown has occurred. Our bodies have changed, and they are now corruptible. This corruptible body is not what it used to be. But at the rapture we're going to put on incorruption. This mortal body that is now subject to death will put on an immortal body.

## WHEN?

In speaking of the rapture, Jesus said, "No man knows the day or hour. . . ." For us to declare some particular date or hour for its occurrence would be a non-Scriptural presumption. If we say we know the hour, we're boasting of knowledge superior to Christ's when He was upon the earth.

Although we do not know the exact time of the rapture, Paul tells us, in 1 Thessalonians 5, "But concerning the times and the seasons, brethren, you have no need that I should write to you. For you yourselves know perfectly that the day of the Lord so comes as a thief in the night. For when they say, 'Peace and safety!' then sudden destruction comes upon them, as labor pains upon a pregnant woman. And they shall not escape. But you, brethren, are not in darkness, so that this day should overtake you as a thief" (1-4). In other words, the rapture shouldn't take us by surprise.

Now you might ask, "What prophecies or conditions are necessary before the rapture of the church takes place?" There are no unfulfilled signs or prophecies. All the necessary prophecies have already been fulfilled. That means the rapture could take place at any time.

Since we know for certain that the rapture will precede the second coming of Jesus, and we know that the prophecies that deal with the second coming are being fulfilled in our world today, we can be sure that the rapture has to be very, very close.

You may ask, "Will that day overtake us as a thief?" We have just read in 1 Thessalonians 5:4 that we are not in darkness that this day should overtake us! God has given to us the warnings that would precede the second coming of Jesus Christ; but as far as the rapture is concerned, Jesus left it as something that could happen at any time. He wants the church to live in the expectancy of His imminent return, and He wants us to do so for four reasons:

First, His imminent return gives urgency to the task that we have of bringing the Gospel to our world. Remembering that His return could be today, and that the fields are ripe for harvest (John 4:35), we set ourselves to the task of sharing the good news of Jesus Christ with a lost and dying world.

Secondly, it is an incentive for pure living. John wrote, "Beloved, now we are children of God; and it has not yet been revealed what we shall be, but we know that when He is revealed, we shall be like Him, for we shall see Him as He is" (1 John 3:2).

John then adds, "And everyone who has this hope in Him purifies himself, just as He is pure" (3:3). The realization that Jesus could come at any moment is a real incentive for pure living. In light of the fact that the Lord might come even today, there are certain things we should do. But first, let me tell you what you shouldn't do. Don't quit your job, sell your house, or see how much money you can borrow, figuring you won't have to pay it back. Jesus said, "Do business till I come" (Luke 19:13).

Thirdly, His imminent return causes us to look up. Jesus said, "Watch therefore, for you do not know what hour your Lord is coming" (Matthew 24:42). Two verses later, He said, "Therefore you also be ready, for the Son of Man is coming at an hour you do not expect."

In Hebrews it is written, "To those who eagerly wait for Him He will appear a second time" (Hebrews 9:28). Amos cried out, "Prepare to meet thy God" (Amos 4:12).

These verses tell us to ready ourselves and watch for His return. They warn us that the time is now to give our hearts to Jesus Christ, who is both ready and willing to forgive us our sins and blot out our transgressions.

And the fourth reason God wants us to live in expectation of His imminent return is that it helps us maintain a right attitude towards the material things of this world. In writing to the Corinthians concerning the coming of the Lord, Paul warns them that the time is short, and reasons that as believers, they should let their every contact with the world be as light as possible. In other words, hang loose. We don't want to get so attached to this world that when the Lord comes for His church, we say, "Wait a minute, Lord." There won't be time for that. And this world can't compare to what He's planned for us.

## SCENE 2: Parables

### WATCH

Concerning His rapture of the church, Jesus said, "Watch and be ready." And He gave a series of parables emphasizing the importance of watching and the importance of being ready. "But as the days of Noah were, so also will the coming of the Son of Man be. For as in the days before the flood, they were eating and drinking, marrying and giving in marriage, until the day that Noah entered the ark," (Matthew 24:37-38). These people were caught by surprise when the flood came. It was business as usual. They weren't expecting the judgment of God to come. And Jesus is saying that's the condition the world will be in when He comes for His church. While the world is going about their normal business, the rapture will catch them by surprise.

Jesus said, "Watch therefore, for you do not know what hour your Lord is coming. But know this, that if the master of the house had known what hour the thief would come, he would have watched and not allowed his house to be broken into. Therefore you also be ready, for the Son of Man is coming at an hour you do not expect" (Matthew 24:42-44). He then spoke of the faithful servant and the evil servant. He said, "Who then is a faithful and wise servant, whom his master made ruler over his household, to give them food in due season? Blessed is that servant whom his master, when he comes, will find so doing" (24:45-46). "But," he said, "if that evil servant says in his heart, 'My master is delaying his coming,' and begins to beat his fellow servants, and to eat and drink with the drunkards, the master of that servant will come on a day when he is not looking for him and at an hour that he is not aware of, and will cut him in two and appoint him his portion with the hypocrites" (24:48-51).

In Matthew 25:2-6, Jesus also spoke of the ten virgins, five who were wise and five who were foolish. They waited for the bridegroom to come, but when the call finally went out, they were sleeping. "Behold, the bridegroom is coming." Awaking, they began to trim their lamps, but the five foolish virgins found that the oil in their lamp was depleted. And so they sought to get the oil from the wise virgins, who told them, "No, if we give to you, we won't have enough for ourselves. You'd better go see if you can buy some." While they were away trying to buy the oil, the bridegroom came, and we read that "those who were ready went in with him to the wedding; and the door was shut." So you see, in each of the situations that Jesus described, the importance of watching was evident, because the rapture could happen at any time and you won't be forewarned. Thus, you need to be ready; you need to be watching. When the foolish virgins returned and sought entry, it was not given to them. Matthew 25:11-12 reads, "Afterward the other virgins came also, saying, 'Lord, Lord, open to us!' But he answered and said, 'Assuredly, I say to you, I do not know you.'" Jesus warns, "Watch therefore, for you know neither the day nor the hour in which the Son of Man is coming."

In Hebrews 9:28 we read, ". . . So Christ was offered once to bear the sins of many. To those who eagerly wait for Him He will appear a second time, apart from sin, for salvation." *Those who eagerly wait for Him.* The Lord expects us and wants us to be watching for Him. He expects and wants us to be ready when He comes.

## SCENE 3: The Unveiling of the Church

The book of Revelation was given to the Apostle John to provide us with a chronology of future events. The Greek word for "revelation" is *apocalypse,* which means "the unveiling." Through this revelation, God is unveiling the future to John.

The book of Revelation is divided into three parts. Revelation 1:19 explains those three parts. "Write the things which you have seen, and the things which are, and the things which will take place after this."

In chapter one, John writes the vision he had of the glorified Christ, who stands in the midst of His churches, holding the pastors in His right hand. Chapters 2 and 3 describe the things which are — the things of the church, the things of church history. In these chapters, Jesus addresses the seven churches. The chronological history of the church is demonstrated in the events that took place in and through these seven churches.

As we look closely at each of these churches, we see a common thread. Though some receive commendations and some receive rebuke, each church is encouraged to listen to what the Spirit has to say to them — and special promises are given to all those who heed and overcome.

## EPHESUS: THE APOSTOLIC CHURCH

As Jesus addresses these individual churches, He first commends them for the good (if any) that they had done. To the church of Ephesus, He first acknowledges their works, their labor, their patience, and the fact that they showed discernment toward those who were false apostles.

> TO THE ANGEL OF THE CHURCH OF EPHESUS WRITE, THESE THINGS SAYS HE WHO HOLDS THE SEVEN STARS IN HIS RIGHT HAND, WHO WALKS IN THE MIDST OF THE SEVEN GOLDEN LAMP-STANDS: I KNOW YOUR WORKS, YOUR LABOR, YOUR PATIENCE, AND THAT YOU CANNOT BEAR THOSE WHO ARE EVIL. AND YOU HAVE TESTED THOSE WHO SAY THEY ARE APOSTLES AND ARE NOT, AND HAVE FOUND THEM LIARS; AND YOU HAVE PERSEVERED AND HAVE PATIENCE, AND HAVE LABORED FOR MY NAME'S SAKE AND HAVE NOT BECOME WEARY (REVELATION 2:1-3).

This was a church that worked for the Lord. And this is a good thing. We know, of course, that we are not made righteous by our works. But when a person is genuinely saved, the evidence of that salvation will be manifested in their works. God declares that He knows their works — their labor, their patience.

He also commends them for refusing to compromise by tolerating evil. One of the weaknesses of the church today is the fact that we have begun to tolerate evil practices. Some groups try to silence the church from speaking against their ungodly, unscriptural lifestyle. They put pressure on the church to accept their lives of sin. Sadly, many churches do just that. But the church of Ephesus was not afraid to speak against evil. Ephesus was not a compromising church.

These are great traits within a church. From the outside, it appeared to be a well organized, functioning church. Everything seemed to be in order. Looking at it, you'd say, "My, that is really a great church. Look at the works. Look at the labor. Look at all their social work and the influence they have in the community." But the Lord had more to say.

NEVERTHELESS I HAVE THIS AGAINST YOU, THAT YOU HAVE LEFT YOUR FIRST LOVE ( REV- ELATION 2:4).

The greatest characteristic of the Christian life is love. Nothing excels love. Love is so vital that God commanded us to love Him with all our heart, mind, soul and strength, and to love one another even as He has loved us.

So even though Ephesus went through all the right motions, they lacked the one vital emotion. Whatever service we render to God, whatever works we do for Him, our motivation must be love. In this, the church at Ephesus was failing.

And what was the remedy? God laid out the steps clearly: remember, repent, and return.

> REMEMBER THEREFORE FROM WHERE YOU HAVE FALLEN; REPENT AND DO THE FIRST WORKS (REVELATION 2:5).

"Do the first works." Some of you, like the church at Ephesus, have left your first love. If you would go back and start doing those first things again — lay off the TV and spend more time devouring God's Word like you once did — you'd find that flame reignited in your heart. You'd find your first love again. The consequences of continuing on a loveless path are disastrous. "Or else," God said, "I will come to you quickly and remove your lampstand from its place — unless you repent" (2:5).

Jesus wants nothing to do with a legal relationship. He never wants you to feel duty-bound. Instead of feeling, "I've got to do this for the Lord," He wants you to desire to work because you love Him. "I won't stay in a loveless church," He warns. He's not interested in all of the works, the labor, the patience, or the discernment if love is not the motive behind it.

Then the Lord commends them again. "But this you have, that you hate the deeds of the Nicolaitans, which I also hate" (Revelation 2:6).

The word *Nicolaitan* is made up of two Greek words: *Nikol*, which is the priest; *Laity* or *laocean*, which is the laity or the priesthood over the laity: the establishing of a priesthood.

What this tells us is that the priesthood had already begun to be established. "Holy men" had already begun to step between people and God. While it's good for us to intercede for one another, it's unnecessary and even wrong for us to try to be intermediaries for one another. Only Jesus stands as a mediator between God and man. And He hates when anyone stands as a gate between you and your Father. The church at Ephesus hated that, too, which earned them this commendation.

Then Jesus gave the call: He who has an ear, let him hear what the Spirit says to the churches and the special promise to the overcomers: "To him who overcomes I will give to eat of the tree from life, which is in the midst of the Paradise of God" (Revelation 2:7).

117

From an historic viewpoint, the church of Ephesus was the original apostolic church — the early New Testament church. As John writes this letter, the church is only around fifty years old, and we see that problems had already begun to develop. And things only get worse as we progress through church history.

Except for the church as described in the book of Acts — which did reach the whole world with the gospel within thirty years of its birth and demonstrated its love and concern for one another — you don't find the church throughout history fulfilling its purpose as God intended. The history of the church is really a history of failure — failure to be and do what God would have the church be and do. Just fifty years after Jesus' resurrection, Jesus is writing to the churches rebuking them. To five of the seven churches named, He calls for repentance. So if you want to see God's true model for the church, you have to go all the way back to the beginning of the church — all the way to the book of Acts.

## SMYRNA: THE PERSECUTED CHURCH

Smyrna represents church history from about AD 100-315. During this period, the church was under severe persecution by the Roman government. John Fox in his *Book of Martyrs* estimates that five million Christians were martyred for their faith during this time.

"And to the angel of the church in Smyrna write, 'These things says the First and the Last, who was dead, and came to life'" (Revelation 2:8). Smyrna is the modern day Izmir, one of the great cities in Turkey. The believers in this beautiful seaport town were to undergo tremendous persecution. And so Jesus identifies Himself as "the First and the Last, who was dead, and came to life." Because many of them face martyrdom, Jesus identifies Himself as one who was put to death but who came to life again. He gives them the hope of resurrection.

"I know your works, tribulation, and poverty (but you are rich)" (Revelation 2:9). Most of the Christians in the early church were slaves. If a wealthy person embraced Christianity, the government would seize their property and wealth. So the people were rather poor financially. But they were rich in the thing that mattered most.

You know, you can't measure your riches by your bank account. That's not a true measure of wealth. The true measure of riches is kept in heaven. It's the eternal treasure you've sent ahead. Some who have been rich on earth will be paupers in heaven. Others who were poor on earth will be rich in heaven. That's why Jesus warned us to not lay up treasures on earth "where moth and rust destroy and where thieves break in and steal" (Matthew 6:19-20), but instead to lay up our treasure in heaven.

"And I know the blasphemy of those who say they are Jews and are not, but are a synagogue of Satan" (Revelation 2:9). Much of the persecution of the early church was prompted by Jews. That's just a fact of history. The apostle Paul was constantly plagued by the Jews, who stirred up all kinds of problems for him. Wherever he went with the gospel, they attacked him. But Jesus is pointing out here that some who say they are Jews are not Jews at all. They are the synagogue of Satan.

In John 8, Jesus was talking with the Jews and they tried to defend themselves by saying, "Abraham is our father." He answered, "If you were Abraham's children, you would do the work of Abraham. . . You are of your father the Devil, and the desires of your father you want to do" (John 8:39, 44). At that, they picked up stones to throw at Him. Having the name "Jew" did not mean they did the work of God. In fact, they were actually fighting against the things of God.

Jesus then encouraged the church at Smyrna: "Do not fear any of those things which you are about to suffer. Indeed, the Devil is about to throw some of you into prison, that you may be tested, and you will have tribulation ten days. Be faithful until death, and I will give you the crown of life. He who has an ear, let him hear what the Spirit says to the churches. He who overcomes shall not be hurt by the second death" (Revelation 2:10-11).

This ten-day long tribulation is thought to refer to the ten emperors of Rome that instigated and carried out the great persecution against the church. Paul was beheaded under Nero's reign between AD 64-68. Domitian exiled John to the island of Patmos in AD 95-96. Trajan burned Ignatius at the stake (AD 104-117). Polycarp was martyred under the rule of Marcus Aurelius (AD 161-180). Other brutal dictators followed: Severus (AD 200-211), Maximinus (AD 235-237), Decius (AD 250-253), Valerian (AD 257-260), Aurelian (AD 270-275). The worst of all was Diocletian from AD 303-313.

"Fear not," Jesus told the church at Smyrna. In Matthew 10:28, He gave the same warning. "Do not fear those who kill the body but cannot kill the soul." Though we may suffer persecution on earth, our reward is waiting in heaven. Though we may suffer for His name's sake here, we have the hope of eternal glory, and the crown of life.

## PERGAMOS: THE COMPROMISED CHURCH

The church at Pergamos corresponds to the state church developed by Constantine. This period, between AD 315-505, was one of the most tragic periods of church history because it was here where the world became a part of the church. When Constantine made Christianity a state religion — practically legislating Christianity — the marriage of church and state created a great deal of evil.

The opening words of Jesus' address to Pergamos are telling. "And to the angel of the church in Pergamos write, 'These things says He who has the sharp two-edged sword'" (Revelation 2:12). This description echoes the description of Jesus in Revelation chapter 1: "Out of His mouth went a sharp two-edged sword" (1:16). Hebrews 4:12 tells us that "The word of God is living and powerful, and sharper than any two-edged sword, piercing even to the dividing of soul and spirit, and of joints and marrow, and is a discerner of the thoughts and intents of the heart." So when Jesus begins this letter by describing Himself as one who has a sharp two-edged sword, you know that judgment is coming.

> I KNOW YOUR WORKS, AND WHERE YOU DWELL,
> WHERE SATAN'S THRONE IS (REVELATION 2:13).

Pergamos was a luxurious city, filled with pagan temples. Most of the pagan religions involved satanic worship. Though Pergamos existed in the midst of that satanic worship, Jesus commends them for holding onto Him.

"And you hold fast to My name, and did not deny My faith even in the days in which Antipas was My faithful martyr, who was killed among you, where Satan dwells" (Revelation 2:13).

They held fast to their faith, despite the evil practices around them; despite the threat of persecution.

> BUT I HAVE A FEW THINGS AGAINST YOU, BECAUSE YOU HAVE THERE THOSE WHO HOLD THE DOCTRINE OF BALAAM, WHO TAUGHT BALAK TO PUT A STUMBLING BLOCK BEFORE THE CHILDREN OF ISRAEL, TO EAT THINGS SAC-RIFICED TO IDOLS, AND TO COMMIT SEXUAL IMMORALITY (REVELATION 2:14).

The "doctrine of Balaam" refers to the account in Numbers chapters 22-24, when the king of Moab, Balak, promised a rich reward to the prophet Balaam if he would curse the children of Israel. When Balaam was unable to speak a curse against the Israelites, he instead instructed Balak in how he might bring down the people. "Cause the people to turn from God and to begin to worship idols," he suggested, "and then their God, who is a jealous God, will smite them." To this end, Balak instructed his women to lure the children of Israel into sexual sin and idol worship.

In a nutshell, the doctrine of Balaam is idol worship. But in a broader sense, it could be described as worshiping God in unprescribed ways. The Moabites worshiped Aphrodite, the fertility goddess, through sexual ritual. They introduced this practice to the children of Israel, who participated willingly. But there are other ways to worship God in unprescribed ways. One such way is through the development of the priesthood and the reverence of icons. This is what began in Pergamos — the hierarchy of priesthood and the inclusion of sacred relics and icons.

But there was more. "Thus you also have those who hold the doctrine of the Nicolaitans, which thing I hate" (2:15). The church in Ephesus hated the work of the Nicolaitans, but some in Pergamos approved. "Repent, or else I will come to you quickly and will fight against them with the sword of My mouth" (Revelation 2:16).

And then, as He does with each church, Jesus urges them to heed the Spirit, and gives a promise to those who overcome. "He who has an ear, let him hear what the Spirit says to the churches. To him who overcomes I will give some of the hidden manna to eat. And I will give him a white stone, and on the stone a new name written which no one knows except him who receives it" (Revelation 2:17).

God has a new name for you — a special name that no one knows except the Lord. That new name is probably associated with the future and all that God has in store for you.

The following four churches have historical counter-parts, but each continues to today. In reading about the churches of Thyatira or Sardis, the readers with various traditional denominational backgrounds could easily become upset. The point is not that Jesus is picking on any one particular church, but that He's exposing all the faults and weaknesses that exist in the church today and have existed in the church throughout history.

## THYATIRA: THE PAGAN CHURCH

Thyatira represents church history from AD 500 to the present time. When we get into the descriptions of these four churches, all exist to the present time.

> AND TO THE ANGEL OF THE CHURCH IN THYAT-IRA WRITE, 'THESE THINGS SAYS THE SON OF GOD, WHO HAS EYES LIKE A FLAME OF FIRE, AND HIS FEET LIKE FINE BRASS (REVELATION 2:18).

Back in chapter one, Jesus was described as having eyes like a flame of fire and feet like brass glowing in the heat.

In the Scriptures, brass symbolizes judgment. When Israel's murmuring brought a plague of fiery serpents upon them — serpents which began to bite and kill the people — God commanded Moses to make a brass serpent and raise it on a pole, so that when the people looked on it, they would be healed of the deadly bite. The brass serpent on the pole was a symbol that their sin had been judged. The one who looked on the serpent would live.

Jesus said, "As Moses lifted up the serpent in the wilderness, even so must the Son of Man be lifted up, that whoever believes in Him should not perish but have eternal life" (John 3:14, 15). Our sins were judged on the cross. And so the "feet of fine brass" refers to the judgment He will bring against this pagan system.

I KNOW YOUR WORKS, LOVE, SERVICE, FAITH, AND YOUR PATIENCE; AND AS FOR YOUR WORKS, THE LAST ARE MORE THAN THE FIRST (REVELATION 2:19).

When I read this, I think of Mother Theresa and her tremendous work in the slums of India. I think of how many have devoted their lives in Christian service working among the poor. Jesus sees every sacrifice of these faithful servants. And, of course, the Catholic Church has taught its people to have tremendous faith in God and in the virgin birth of Jesus Christ. Those are the pluses, but there are a few problems, too.

> NEVERTHELESS I HAVE A FEW THINGS AGAINST YOU, BECAUSE YOU ALLOW THAT WOMAN JEZE-BEL, WHO CALLS HERSELF A PROPHETESS, TO TEACH AND SEDUCE MY SERVANTS TO COMMIT SEXUAL IMMORALITY AND EAT THINGS SACRI-FICED TO IDOLS (REVELATION 2:20).

Jezebel was the Old Testament wife of King Ahab. It was Jezebel who brought the worship of Baal unto the Northern Kingdom of Israel and enticed them to commit spiritual fornication.

The church is to be married to Jesus Christ even as Israel was to be married to God. Being married to Jesus Christ means we're to be totally faithful to Him, worshiping Him alone. The worship of anything else constitutes spiritual fornication. Now, God told the children of Israel, "You shall have no other gods before Me. You shall not make for yourself a carved image, or any likeness *of anything* that *is* in heaven above, or that *is* in the earth beneath, or that *is* in the water under the earth; you shall not bow down to them nor serve them" (Exodus 20:3-5). In other words, God prohibited icons.

Jezebel introduced the idols of Baal to the Israelites. People had them in their homes and looked to them for guidance. This was the introduction of images, or idols. We see them throughout the different denominations — likenesses of Jesus, likenesses of Mary, likenesses of the saints venerated by the people.

The Lord said, "And I gave her time to repent of her sexual immorality, and she did not repent. Indeed I will cast her into a sickbed, and those who commit adultery with her into great tribulation, unless they repent of their deeds. I will kill her children with death, and all the churches shall know that I am He who searches the minds and hearts. And I will give to each one of you according to your works" (Revelation 2:21-23).

Notice that unless there is repentance and a turning from their deeds, this church will enter into the great tribulation period. But the inference is that if they do repent, they'll escape the great tribulation.

NOW TO YOU I SAY, AND TO THE REST IN THYATIRA, AS MANY AS DO NOT HAVE THIS DOCTRINE, WHO HAVE NOT KNOWN THE DEPTHS OF SATAN, AS THEY SAY, I WILL PUT ON YOU NO OTHER BURDEN (REVELATION 2:24).

It's a matter of fact that at times during this period of history, the position of pope was auctioned off to the highest bidder. It's undeniable. The position of pope was desecrated many times. But it's also true that this period of church history produced many wonderful, godly saints — men who loved the Lord completely. And there are, within the Catholic Church today, many marvelous people who do love our Lord Jesus Christ. Jesus addresses such overcomers:

> BUT HOLD FAST WHAT YOU HAVE TILL I COME. AND HE WHO OVERCOMES, AND KEEPS MY WORKS UNTIL THE END, TO HIM I WILL GIVE POWER OVER THE NATIONS — HE SHALL RULE THEM WITH A ROD OF IRON; THEY SHALL BE DASHED TO PIECES LIKE THE POTTER'S VESSELS — AS I ALSO HAVE RECEIVED FROM MY FATHER; AND I WILL GIVE HIM THE MORNING STAR. HE WHO HAS AN EAR, LET HIM HEAR WHAT THE SPIRIT SAYS TO THE CHURCHES (REVELATION 2:25-29).

He who loves us and gave Himself for us promises that we will be a kingdom of priests. These overcomers will reign with the Lord during the thousand-year millennial reign of Christ and will enforce righteous rule upon the earth.

## SARDIS: THE DEAD CHURCH

> AND TO THE ANGEL OF THE CHURCH IN SARDIS
> WRITE, THESE THINGS SAYS HE WHO HAS THE
> SEVEN SPIRITS OF GOD AND THE SEVEN STARS:
> I KNOW YOUR WORKS, THAT YOU HAVE A NAME
> THAT YOU ARE ALIVE, BUT YOU ARE DEAD (REV-
> ELATION 3:1).

Not a wonderful introduction. Historically, the church at Sardis represents the period of the Protestant Reformation, from the 1500s to the present time. The Reformation began with a mighty move of God's Spirit, and is full of great names such as Luther, Calvin, Knox, Zwingli, and Huss. It was a time of renewed love for the Scriptures, yet it soon developed into an organizational structure. The Lord takes issue with their works. "Be watchful, and strengthen the things which remain, that are ready to die, for I have not found your works perfect before God" (Revelation 3:2).

The Protest Reformation was not a total reformation. The church brought many of the Babylonian traditions from the Catholic Church into the Protestant church, and thus, it soon became dead. Many of the great denominations that were once alive in the things of God have become dead today, with a dead orthodoxy.

For example, infant baptism is not taught in the Scriptures. It was an invention of the Catholic Church, borrowed from the Babylonian religion. The Catholic Church also borrowed pagan holidays, which they renamed with Christian names. Though Christmas is said to be the birth of Christ, it is actually based around the Roman celebration of Saturnalia, which originated from an ancient Babylonian celebration of the birth of Tammuz to his mother Semiramis. Tammuz was worshiped as a god; so therefore, you have the mother and child. Despite the fact that the Scriptures do not tell us the actual date of Christ's birth — and it would be highly unlikely for the shepherds to be watching their flock by night anytime later than October — the Catholic Church adopted the celebration of Semiramis and decided to celebrate Christ's birth on that date.

Easter is yet another example. The word *Easter* comes from the name of the pagan goddess Ashtarte. At the spring solstice, the pagans celebrated new life by coloring eggs, which represent perpetuated life. The Catholic Church adopted that ritual and even took the name *Easter* from *Ashtarte.*

Much of the Babylonian influence was carried over into the Protestant church at the Reformation, and thus the Lord said, "I have not found your works perfect or complete before God." There wasn't a complete break. And so the Lord said, "Remember therefore how you have received and heard; hold fast and repent. Therefore if you will not watch, I will come upon you as a thief, and you will not know what hour I will come upon you" (Revelation 3:3).

It would be good for the churches that came out of the Protestant Reformation to go back and remember their origins. It would be good to remember when Luther stepped out and said, "The just shall live by faith," and when he shared that "The Spirit and the gifts are ours," and spoke about the gifts and the power of the Spirit. It would be good to remember John Knox, and John Wesley. Unfortunately, some of these men would not be welcomed in their own churches today.

"You have a few names even in Sardis who have not defiled their garments; and they shall walk with Me in white, for they are worthy" (Revelation 3:4). Not all the churches that have come out of the Reformation are dead. I think of some of the marvelous ministers in the Lutheran church and in the Presbyterian church who have ministered through the years. But unfortunately, when you look at the church as a whole, it has become cold, formal and ritualistic. It has a name that it is alive, but it is ready to die.

And then, Jesus gives a promise to the overcomers, "He who overcomes shall be clothed in white garments, and I will not blot out his name from the Book of Life; but I will confess his name before My Father and before His angels. He who has an ear, let him hear what the Spirit says to the churches" (Revelation 3:5-6).

Those who hold very strict to the idea of eternal security, that once you have received Jesus Christ or have been saved that you can never be lost no matter what you do, have great difficulty with this verse. It is interesting to read their commentaries and see how they try to skate around the words of Jesus. If it is not possible for a person's name to be blotted out of the Book of Life, then why would Jesus have said this? His words would be totally meaningless. Why would He even make such a suggestion unless such a thing was possible?

Those who overcome will be clothed in white, and their names will be confessed before God and His angels.

## PHILADELPHIA: THE BELOVED CHURCH

The church in Philadelphia lasted until about AD 1300, when the Turks destroyed the church and murdered the remaining Christians there. About all that remains of the ancient city of Philadelphia are the ruins of a Byzantine chapel.

AND TO THE ANGEL OF THE CHURCH IN PHILA-
DELPHIA WRITE, THESE THINGS SAYS *HE WHO
IS HOLY, HE WHO IS TRUE, HE WHO HAS THE KEY
OF DAVID, HE WHO OPENS AND NO ONE SHUTS,
AND SHUTS AND NO ONE OPENS* (REVELATION
3:7).

The Lord introduces Himself now as the One who has
the key of David, the One who can open and no man
shuts; shuts and no man opens. He says, "I know your
works. See, I have set before you an open door, and no
one can shut it" (Revelation 3:8).

God so often leads us by opening a door of opportunity for us. And He often stops us by closing the door.
I don't believe when God closes a door we should try
and force it open or break it down. I've learned to just
accept closed doors as well as I have open doors. So if
God closes one door, look for another. Don't try and
break it down. God has something else in mind. That's a
great way to live. To just let God open or shut the doors
before you. It takes all the pressure off.

"For you have a little strength, have kept My word, and
have not denied My name" (Revelation 3:8). The church
of Philadelphia is *the* church in the last days — and it's
not a denomination. This is a church that doesn't have

great strength, only a little strength. But it's a church that has faithfully kept the Word of God. There are a few denominational churches that have kept faithfully teaching the Word of God, but not too many are left today in which the pastors teach the Scriptures verse by verse, line by line, chapter by chapter.

This little church is never going to become powerful or strong. It's never going to turn the world upside down. But it will continue to faithfully keep God's Word and it will not deny His name.

God loves that about the church of Philadelphia. "Indeed I will make *those* of the synagogue of Satan, who say they are Jews and are not, but lie — indeed I will make them come and worship before your feet, and to know that I have loved you" (Revelation 3:9).

One day, the Jewish people will recognize that their forefathers made the greatest and most tragic mistake in the history of the nation when they failed to recognize that Jesus was the promised Messiah. That will take place during the great tribulation period when the man that they hail as their Messiah turns out to be the Antichrist. When he stands in the rebuilt temple declaring that he is God, they will recognize then that they have been deceived and will turn to Jesus Christ in great numbers.

And they will recognize the truth of the church. So the Lord said, "I will make them come and worship before your feet, and to know that I have loved you."

Now the Lord makes a comforting promise, "Because you have kept My command to persevere, I also will keep you from the hour of trial which shall come upon the whole world, to test those who dwell on the earth" (Revelation 3:10).

The hour of trial, of course, refers to the great tribulation. The world will go through a bloodbath during this horrific period. It will be a time of tribulation such as the world has never seen before, nor will ever see again.

As John received his vision from God about the details of the tribulation, he saw them through the eyes of a man who lived 2,000 years ago and who knew nothing of the weapons of warfare that would be developed after his time. He was a man who never saw an airplane, never saw a tank, never saw the weapons of modern warfare and the means of destroying mankind. Without knowledge of those things, he does his best to describe them with items that would be familiar to him at that time.

But as we get into the imagery and the descriptions, we can see how they do apply to many of the modern weapons and modern warfare we have today — even to the atomic and nuclear bombs. We get a glimpse of the mass destruction of humanity that is going to take place when God pours out His wrath and His judgment upon this world. Nothing we've read about in our history books can match what's going to happen in this time of judgment — not the Holocaust, not wars, not the Flood, not even the destruction of Sodom and Gomorrah when God rained fire and brimstone from heaven. But because they have kept the Word of His patience, God gives the church of Philadelphia this blessed promise: "I will keep you from the hour of trial which shall come upon the whole world, to test those who dwell on the earth" (Revelation 3:10).

BEHOLD, I AM COMING QUICKLY! HOLD FAST WHAT YOU HAVE, THAT NO ONE MAY TAKE YOUR CROWN. HE WHO OVERCOMES, I WILL MAKE HIM A PILLAR IN THE TEMPLE OF MY GOD, AND HE SHALL GO OUT NO MORE. AND I WILL WRITE ON HIM THE NAME OF MY GOD AND THE NAME OF THE CITY OF MY GOD, THE NEW JERUSALEM, WHICH COMES DOWN OUT OF HEAVEN FROM MY GOD. AND *I WILL WRITE ON HIM* MY NEW NAME. HE WHO HAS AN EAR,

LET HIM HEAR WHAT THE SPIRIT SAYS TO THE CHURCHES (REVELATION 3:11-13).

He is coming quickly. His return will be so quick, it will happen in a twinkling of an eye. And so the church of Philadelphia is urged to hold on to what they have, remembering His soon return.

Paul said, "I have fought the good fight, I have finished the race, I have kept the faith. Finally, there is laid up for me the crown of righteousness, which the Lord, the righteous Judge, will give to me on that Day, and not to me only but also to all who have loved His appearing" (2 Timothy 4:7-8). All who love His appearing will be given a crown of righteousness that will be given unto us. "Hold fast what you have, that no one may take your crown."

## LAODICEA: THE LUKEWARM CHURCH

AND TO THE ANGEL OF THE CHURCH OF THE LAODICEANS WRITE, THESE THINGS SAYS THE AMEN, THE FAITHFUL AND TRUE WITNESS, THE BEGINNING OF THE CREATION OF GOD (REVELATION 3:14).

In addressing the church of Laodicea, Jesus describes Himself as the faithful and true witness. What does that mean? It means that Jesus is a true witness of God. That is, if you want to know what God is like, you can look at Jesus and understand exactly what God is like. Jesus told the Jews, "I and My Father are one" (John 10:30). His life was a witness to us of who God is.

> I KNOW YOUR WORKS, THAT YOU ARE NEITHER COLD NOR HOT. I COULD WISH YOU WERE COLD OR HOT. SO THEN, BECAUSE YOU ARE LUKE-WARM, AND NEITHER COLD NOR HOT, I WILL VOMIT YOU OUT OF MY MOUTH (REVELATION 3:15-16).

Today, Laodicea is in ruins. But when it was in existence, it had an interesting water system. Two sluices brought water from afar: one brought ice-cold water from the mountain snow; the other brought hot water from a far-off hot spring. The problem was, by the time the hot water reached Laodicea — a distance of some five miles — the once-steaming water was merely luke-warm. Now, most people like hot water. Some people like ice-cold water. But very few people like lukewarm water. Such was the case of the church in Laodicea. They were neither hot nor cold. They were just luke-warm. They weren't on fire for the Lord; neither were they completely apostate. They went to church, but their position was, "I can take it or leave it."

Jesus doesn't want a take-it-or-leave-it relationship with you. He wants a full, right-on relationship with you. And to the church of Laodicea, Jesus said, "Because you are lukewarm, neither cold nor hot, I will spew you out of my mouth."

"Because you say, 'I am rich, have become wealthy, and have need of nothing' — and do not know that you are wretched, miserable, poor, blind, and naked" (Revelation 3:17). *Because you say.* This church believes certain things about itself. But what matters is not what we think about ourselves, but what God thinks. They saw themselves in one light; God saw them in another.

This church saw itself as rich and in need of nothing. I can't help but think again of some denominations that are extremely wealthy. Some cults also fall into this category. These churches have become so large and so well financed that they may feel completely independent of God.

To this modern apostate church, the Lord said, "You are, in reality, wretched, miserable, poor, blind and naked." You're stripped. You have nothing. This is how God views them — quite a contrast to how they view themselves. But God is so gracious and so patient. "I counsel you to buy from Me gold refined in the fire, that you may be rich; and white garments, that you may be clothed, *that* the shame of your nakedness may not be revealed; and anoint your eyes with eye salve, that you may see" (Revelation 3:18).

Interestingly enough, Laodicea was the center of a pharmaceutical firm that made eye salve. A certain kind of white clay from nearby Hierapolis was thought to have medicinal properties. They would mix the clay with spikenard and sell it all over the Roman world as a miracle eye salve — a medical wonder. The fact is, however, that this same recipe has been tested in recent years and found to have no medicinal value whatsoever. How personal and specific the Lord is in this message: "Anoint your eyes with eye salve, that you may see."

Spiritually this church was blind. And unfortunately that is true of so many people today; they are spiritually blind — blindly following blind leaders. So many of the apostate churches today are hiring gay or lesbian pastors. Many churches deny the infallibility of the Bible, deny the divinity of Jesus Christ, the atoning work of Jesus Christ. You have to wonder, "Why do they even exist?" Well, they exist because they've been left great fortunes and large endowments. They exist because the people are blind to their spiritual condition.

The Lord then gives this warning: "As many as I love, I rebuke and chasten. Therefore be zealous and repent" (Revelation 3:19). The Lord still loves this church, and He will chasten them to bring them to repentance. In Hebrews we read, "My son, do not despise the chastening of the Lord, nor be discouraged when you are rebuked by Him; for whom the Lord loves, He chastens, and scourges every son whom He receives" (Hebrews 12:5-6).

In these last verses, we come, in a sense, to the end of church history. And where do we find the Lord? We find Him outside, knocking at the door. "Behold, I stand at the door and knock. If anyone hears My voice and opens the door, I will come in to him and dine with him, and he with Me" (Revelation 3:20).

Salvation, you see, is an individual manner. Jesus knocks on the door of each heart individually. You're not saved by a religious system. You're not saved because salvation was passed down from your parents. You're saved only when you personally respond to the call of Jesus Christ.

And what does He do when you open that door? He comes in and dines with you. He comes in to have intimate fellowship with you.

In the culture of John's day, eating with another person

signified a deep, intimate relationship. In sharing the same food, you shared the same nourishment. Each of you pulled a hunk of bread from the same loaf. Food was dipped in common bowls, and there wasn't a "no-double-dipping" rule. By the time the meal was over, you had all shared the same germs. To them, the dining experience meant becoming one.

This is why people were so shocked when Jesus ate with sinners and publicans — it meant He was becoming one with them. But nothing has changed there. Jesus still eats with sinners. That's why He wants close, intimate fellowship with you. He wants the two of you to become one. And that can only happen if you respond to His knock.

An artist named Holman Hunt painted a picture entitled *The Light of the World*. It shows Jesus knocking on a door with lantern in hand. When some of Holman's friends came to view the painting he had made, one said, "You've left something out. There's no handle on the door." To which Holman relied, "No, that's not an accident. That was deliberate. You see, the handle is on the inside."

So it is that when the Lord knocks at your heart, the only handle is on your side. If you open it, He will come in.

And then Jesus gives a promise to this seventh church. "To him who overcomes I will grant to sit with Me on My throne, as I also overcame and sat down with My Father on His throne. He who has an ear, let him hear what the Spirit says to the churches" (Revelation 3:21-22).

Today, Jesus is sitting at the throne of God in heaven. And He promises those who overcome that they will be able to sit with Him on that throne. What a gracious God! What a glorious promise!

## AFTER THESE THINGS

Revelation 4:1 begins with the words, "After these things." In the Greek, the word for "after these things" is *metatauta* and it is the same word used in Revelation 1:19, when the Lord said, "Write the things which you have seen, and the things which are, and the things which will take place after this." *Metatauta*. So, chapter 4 opens with the words *metatauta* which should immediately cause you to say, "Wait a minute, we're entering into the third section of the book of Revelation." We're entering into the things which are going to take place "after these things," which is obviously referring to after the things of chapters 2 and 3, the things relating to the church. What's going to happen to the world after the ministry of the church is no longer here, has finished her witness on the earth, and has been raptured into heaven? As we will see in Act III, the world we leave behind us will be thrown into a state of increasing sadness, terror, and devastation.

## THE OPEN DOOR

"After these things I looked, and behold, a door standing open in heaven" (Revelation 4:1). John has been given a glimpse of the church age from his time through to the rapture. He will also be given a glimpse of what will transpire during the great tribulation on earth, and the activity in heaven that corresponds to those events. But before he does, John is first given a peek into heaven, and in this passage, he briefly describes that heavenly scene. There he sees the throne of God, in front of which is a glassy sea. He sees the cherubim, those angels around God's throne who declare, day and night, "Holy, holy, holy, Lord God Almighty, who was and is and is to come" (Revelation 4:8).

John then takes note of twenty-four lesser thrones with twenty-four elders sitting on them. And as the cherubim worship God, declaring His holiness and His eternal nature, these elders fall on their faces, cast their golden crowns on the glassy sea, and declare the worthiness of God to receive glory, honor and power, for, as they declare, He has made all things, and by His will they exist and were created. The King James Version states it this way: "For thou hast created all things, and for thy pleasure they are and were created" (Revelation 4:11).

I'd like to pause there for just a moment. The elders are declaring that God has created all things for His good pleasure. "All things" includes you. You exist for God's good pleasure. In fact, that's the very purpose of your existence. And anything else you might *think* is your purpose actually falls short of God's intended purpose for your existence. You say, "Well, I don't appreciate that." Tough. You can't do anything about it. Well, you can, I guess. You can say, "I'm going to live for my own pleasure. I'm not interested in living for God's pleasure." God will allow you to do that, but I guarantee when you reach the end of the road, you will feel just as Solomon did at the end of his life. You'll be a miserable cynic as you look back at your life. You'll shake your head and say, "Emptiness, emptiness, life is empty and filled with frustrations," because you didn't live for the basic purpose of your existence.

Revelation 5 opens with John observing a scroll with seven seals in God's hand. While he watches, a "strong angel" proclaims with a loud voice, "Who is worthy to open the scroll and to loose its seals?" John sees that there is no man in heaven, in the earth, or under the sea who is worthy to take the scroll and to loose the seals.

It is my opinion that this scroll is the title deed to the earth. When God created this planet, He gave it to man. But when Adam sinned, he forfeited that title. Adam's sin turned the earth over to Satan. In John 12, 14 and 16, Satan is referred to as "the prince of this world." One of the purposes of Jesus' coming to the world was to redeem it back to God. He came for redemption. "The Son of Man," He said, "has come to seek and to save that which was lost, (Luke 19:10). Who can redeem the world? Who is worthy to take the scroll and loose the seals? Surely no mere man was found worthy.

When John saw that there was no man capable of opening the scroll, he began to weep. Perhaps he realized the implication for earth — that it looked like Satan would control the world forever. But one of the elders said to John, "Do not weep. Behold, the Lion of the tribe of Judah, the Root of David, has prevailed to open the scroll and to loose its seven seals" (Revelation 5:5).

At that, John turned and beheld the Lamb, standing in the midst of the throne, the four creatures, and the worshiping elders. The Bible says, in describing the Lamb, that it looked "as though it had been slain, having seven horns and seven eyes, which are the seven Spirits of God sent out into all the earth. Then He came and took the scroll out of the right hand of Him who sat on the throne" (5:6-7).

147

When the Lamb took the scroll from the right hand of the Father, John tells us that the twenty-four elders fell before Him. And each had a harp and a bowl of incense, which, we're told, "are the prayers of the saints" (Revelation 5:8). How often have you prayed, "Your kingdom come. Your will be done on earth as it is in heaven?" The church has prayed that prayer for almost two thousand years. But here in Revelation the time has come when the kingdoms of this world will become the kingdoms of our Lord and of His Messiah and He shall reign forever and ever. And so the elders come forth with these little vials, the prayers of the saints, which they offer before God. Does it surprise you to know that your prayers rise to God like a sweet-smelling incense? It makes you want to pray more, doesn't it?

And then the saints sang a new song. "You are worthy to take the scroll, and to open its seals; for You were slain, and have redeemed us to God by Your blood out of every tribe and tongue and people and nation, and have made us kings and priests to our God; and we shall reign on the earth" (Revelation 5:9-10).

Look again at the lyrics of that song. It's saying, "You, Jesus, are worthy to take the scroll because You were slain. You've redeemed us by Your blood out of every kindred, tongue, people, and nation."

Some scholars argue that the lyrics of the song should read, "For You were slain, and have redeemed *them* to God." In only a handful of the old manuscripts from the Alexandrian School of Texts, the text reads "them" instead of "us." However, the vast majority — over 1,000 old manuscripts of the Majority Text, or Textus Receptus — reads as translated in the New King James Version, "redeemed *us* to God," which is rightfully translated.

That's a song only the church can sing. That isn't the song of Israel. In the Old Testament we have the song of Moses, which is about God delivering Israel out of the bondage of Egypt. But this song, like the church, is from every nation, every ethnic group. They're singing of the worthiness of the Lamb to take the scroll and to loose the seals because He was slain and He has redeemed us by His blood. Since only the church can sing this song, and it's being sung in heaven, the church is clearly in heaven. We are there rejoicing in the worthiness of Jesus to take the scroll and loose the seals.

It is interesting that the great judgment of God — the great tribulation — will not begin until Jesus begins to break the seals on this scroll, which means that the church will be in heaven during the time of the great tribulation here on earth. In this song, the verse is exclusive to the church, but when we get to the chorus, a hundred million angels will lift their voices with ours. Though they can't sing of redemption, angels can certainly sing about the worthiness of the Lamb to receive His power and glory. That reminds me of the old song, *Holy, Holy, is What the Angels Sing*:

> *There is singing up in Heaven such as we have never known,*
> *Where the angels sing the praises of the Lamb upon the throne,*
> *Their sweet harps are ever tuneful, and their voices always clear,*
> *Oh, that we might be more like them while we serve the Master here!*

> *Holy, holy, is what the angels sing,*
> *And I expect to help them make the courts of heaven ring;*
> *But when I sing redemption's story, they will fold their wings,*
> *For angels never felt the joys that our salvation brings.*

> *But I hear another anthem, blending voices clear and strong,*
> *"Unto Him who hath redeemed us and hath bought us," is the song;*
> *We have come through tribulation to this land so fair and bright,*
> *In the fountain freely flowing He hath made our garments white.*

*Then the angels stand and listen, for they cannot join the song,*

*Like the sound of many waters, by that happy, blood-washed throng,*

*For they sing about great trials, battles fought and vict'ries won,*

*And they praise their great Redeemer, who hath said to them, "Well done."*

*So, although I'm not an angel, yet I know that over there*

*I will join a blessed chorus that the angels cannot share;*

*I will sing about my Savior, who upon dark Calvary*

*Freely pardoned my transgressions, died to set a sinner free.[6]*

Our voices, mingled with those of a hundred million angels. What an amazing choir that will be!

In speaking to His disciples about the great tribulation that would come upon the earth, Jesus said, "Watch therefore, and pray always that you may be counted worthy to escape all these things that will come to pass, and to stand before the Son of Man" (Luke 21:36). *Pray that you may be counted worthy.* I do not believe that every one who knows of Jesus is going up in the rapture, but only

---

[6] Oatman, Jr., J. and Sweney, J., "Holy, Holy, is What the Angels Sing." c. 1894.

those who are ready. Jesus made that perfectly clear in His repeated warnings to watch and be ready.

## SCENE 4: The Three Camps

Why is there so much confusion concerning the timing of the rapture? Why the three camps: pre-trib, mid-trib, and post-trib ?

The mistake and the confusion regarding the church's place in the last times arise out of a misunderstanding of God's full prophecies concerning the nation of Israel. Israel will go through the great tribulation. This will be the time of Jacob's troubles spoken of in Jeremiah 30:7, "Alas! For that day is great, so that none is like it; and it is the time of Jacob's trouble, but he shall be saved out of it." This will be the time when, as Jesus said, "For I say to you, you shall see Me no more till you say, 'Blessed is He who comes in the name of the LORD!'" (Matthew 23:39).

After the great tribulation period Israel will say, "Oh, blessed is He Who comes in the name of the Lord!" Jesus shall return again with His church at His second coming. The prophet Zechariah said, "And one shall say unto him, 'What are these wounds in thine hands?' Then he shall answer, 'Those with which I was wounded in the house of my friends'" (Zechariah 13:6). Thus, the glorious first recognition of Jesus as Israel's Messiah is when He comes the second time (after the rapture) with the church to establish His reign upon the earth.

## LOST FOREVER?

Does all this mean that if you miss the rapture, you're going to be lost forever? No. In Revelation, chapter 7, we find that there is a great number in heaven, an innumerable host standing before the throne and before the Lamb. Clothed with white robes, they hold palms in their hands and cry with a loud voice, saying, "Salvation belongs to our God who sits on the throne, and to the Lamb!" All the angels stood around the throne and the elders and the four living creatures, and fell on their faces before the throne and worshiped God, saying: "Amen! Blessing and glory and wisdom, thanksgiving and honor and power and might, be to our God forever and ever. Amen" (7:10-12). Notice that every time they declare these things of God, their praise gets longer. The first two were pretty short, "You are worthy, O Lord, to receive glory and honor and power; for You created all things, and by Your will they exist and were created" (Revelation 4:11). But every time they say this praise, they add to it.

So who are these who are clothed in white robes? Where did they come from? It's an innumerable host, and obviously not the church, because if they were the church,

John would have recognized them as such. But he doesn't. We read that an elder has to explain that, "these are the ones who come out of the great tribulation, and washed their robes and made them white in the blood of the Lamb. Therefore they are before the throne of God, and serve Him day and night in His temple. And He who sits on the throne will dwell among them. They shall neither hunger anymore nor thirst anymore; the sun shall not strike them, nor any heat; for the Lamb who is in the midst of the throne will shepherd them and lead them to living fountains of waters. And God will wipe away every tear from their eyes" (Revelation 7:14-17). These are people who have suffered. These are people who endured all this and more during the great tribulation.

The rapture of the church will be a real late wake up call for a lot of people. I believe that the foolish virgins, those not really walking in the Spirit but walking instead after the flesh, will be left behind when the Bridegroom comes. They will be left to face at least a part of the great tribulation period. When the church is raptured, those who have not made a complete commitment of their lives to Christ, those living in a spiritually luke-warm state, will suddenly realize what has happened and they're going to get deadly serious about their relationship with our Lord. And when the Antichrist orders everyone to receive his mark, in order that they might buy or sell, these will refuse the mark of the Antichrist and thus, will be martyred. These newly dedicated will be saved as though plucked out of the fire.

When the fifth seal is opened, John "saw under the altar the souls of those who had been slain for the word of God and for the testimony which they held. And they cried with a loud voice, saying, 'How long, O Lord, holy and true, until You judge and avenge our blood on those who dwell on the earth?'" Then a white robe was given to each of them; and it was said to them that they should rest a little while longer, until both *the number of* their fellowservants and their brethren, who would be killed as they *were*, was completed" (Revelation 6:9-11). I believe that this group mentioned here now completes the number of those who will be martyred during the great tribulation period and they now have their entrance into heaven in a sub-position to the church. The church is the bride of Christ, the church is with Christ, but these are there in the temple worshiping God day and night, and freed from the problems that they experienced during the great tribulation.

## TAKE HEED

We really don't know when the Lord might come for His church. In Luke's gospel, Jesus talked with His disciples

155

about these events. "But take heed to yourselves, lest your hearts be weighed down with carousing, drunkenness, and cares of this life, and that day come on you unexpectedly. For it will come as a snare on all those who dwell on the face of the whole earth" (Luke 21:34-35). Be careful you're not trapped by the cares of this life, eating and drinking. Take heed to Jesus' warning. He's going to come for His church. He's going to come for His church that is busy doing the will of the Father, but also watching and looking for Jesus. Many will be left.

As is so often the case, there's an easy way to go, and a hard way. The easy way to go is to serve the Lord and be ready when He comes. The hard way to go is to live carelessly now. The hard way is to stop short of making a full commitment, and serve God only when it's convenient for you. To worship only when it's convenient. As a pastor, this attitude is of great concern to me. I see too many people who have settled for a convenient, take-it-or-leave-it relationship with the Lord. A comfort zone is a bad zone to live in, because you can comfort yourself right into complacency.

The rapture is close. Jesus has warned us to watch for Him. Will you be ready when the Lord comes for His church?

## CHURCH SAVED FROM GREAT TRIBULATION

- Romans 8:1
- 1 Thessalonians 1:9, 10
- 2 Peter 2:4-10
- Revelation 3:10, 11

## GOD'S PROMISE

- John 14:1-3

## RAPTURE

- 1 Thessalonians 4:13-18

## RAPTURE TRANSFORMATION

- 1 Corinthians 15:51

## READY FOR THE RAPTURE

- Matthew 24:36-44
- Matthew 25:1-13
- Mark 13:32-37
- Luke 17:26, 27, 34-37
- Luke 21:34-36
- 1 Thessalonians 5:1-11

ACT III

# THE GREAT

# TRIBULATION

## Sorrow

AT THE CLOSE OF ACT II, God has taken His church out of the earth in preparation for judgment. Whereas Act II was a scene of expectancy and anticipation, Act III is one of sorrow, horror, and sadness. The scenes that unfold are tough to read, but the prophecies they contain will tell us more about the unfolding drama of the end times.

### IMAGINE

Can you imagine 50–pound chunks of ice falling out of the sky? Can you conceive of the devastation that would occur from a barrage of hailstones weighing fifty pounds? Where would you hide? How could you be safe? Hailstones that heavy would rip through the roof of your house as if it were paper. They would flatten your automobile. What could stand up under that kind of bombardment?

Can you picture the Sierra Nevada mountain range suddenly dropping to 5,000 feet below sea level? The Pacific Ocean would come rushing in to fill the resulting canyon. How could anyone on the West Coast escape? What would happen to the millions of people living there?

Can you conceive of a time when people couldn't die? Perhaps their bodies would be mangled in a car accident or a plane crash, yet their spirits would refuse to leave. They'd have to remain in that maimed condition for months, waiting and wishing for death.

Such events will take place upon the earth — perhaps soon. God will pour His wrath upon the earth and the people who have rejected His plan of salvation. According to the Bible, the tribulation will be a three-and-a-half year period of angst, horror, and delusion.

## SCENE 1: The Two Tribulations

The fact that a time of great tribulation is coming upon the earth is firmly established in the Scriptures. In

Daniel 12:1 we read, "At that time Michael shall stand up, the great prince who stands watch over the sons of your people; and there shall be a time of trouble, such as never was since there was a nation, even to that time. And at that time your people shall be delivered, every one who is found written in the book." This mention of "the book" is, no doubt, a reference to the Book of Life. What a wonderful promise of deliverance!

In Matthew 24:21–22 Jesus said, "For then there will be great tribulation, such as has not been since the beginning of the world until this time, no, nor ever shall be. And unless those days were shortened, no flesh would be saved; but for the elect's sake those days will be shortened." The "elect" here refers to Israel, as evidenced by the context (verses 16, 20). Both Daniel and Jesus spoke about the same "time of trouble" and day of "great tribulation" to come upon the earth.

The book of Revelation gives us many details about the events that will transpire on earth during this time of great tribulation. Chapter 6 begins with the opening of the seven seals of judgment. The tribulation continues through the seven trumpet judgments and the seven vials of God's wrath that will be poured out. If you want to fully understand what this great tribulation will be like, read Revelation chapters 6 through 19.

It's important to make a clear distinction about tribulations as taught in the Bible. Two types are described: (1) the great tribulation referred to by Jesus and Daniel and detailed by John in the book of Revelation, and (2) the tribulation Jesus promised would come to the church.

Speaking to His disciples in John 16:33, Jesus said, "These things I have spoken to you, that in Me you may have peace. In the world you will have tribulation; but be of good cheer, I have overcome the world." The church will have tribulation in the world. It's important to notice that the "tribulation" faced by the church originates from the world and comes from the world system controlled by Satan. Satan is behind these attacks on the church.

Paul tells us that we're not wrestling against flesh and blood, but against "principalities, against powers, against the rulers of the darkness of this age, against spiritual hosts of wickedness in the heavenly places" (Ephesians 6:12). Spirit forces are warring against the children of God. The source of our tribulation is most definitely the world system governed by Satan.

In contrast to this, the great tribulation that will come upon the earth originates from heaven. During that period, God's wrath is poured out in judgment against those who have chosen sin and rejected Him. When the sixth seal is opened in Revelation 6:12, those on the earth will try to hide. They'll call for the rocks and the mountains to fall upon them to hide them from the wrath of the Lamb, for the Great Day of His wrath has come. They will ask, "Who shall be able to stand?" Revelation 11:18 declares, "Your wrath has come."

In Revelation 14:10 the great tribulation is referred to as the indignation and wrath of God. When the seals are opened in heaven, the angels are given trumpets. As they blow these trumpets, corresponding judgments come upon the earth. The vials from the living creatures are opened by the seven angels, and again corresponding judgments come upon the earth. All these judgments come from God and have their origin in heaven. Psalm 69:20-28 gives a prophecy concerning Jesus. It speaks of His disciples forsaking Him in the hour of need and of vinegar being given to Him for His thirst. It then calls for God to pour out His indignation and His wrathful anger upon those who had persecuted the One whom God had smitten. Indignation is a word used frequently in the Old Testament to describe the time of the great tribulation (Isaiah 26:19-20; Isaiah 34:1-8; Jeremiah 10:10; Daniel 8:19; Nahum 1:5-6; Zephaniah 3:8). Note in Isaiah 66:14 that the hand of the Lord will be known to His children but His indignation to His enemies.

Paul tells us in Romans 2:6-8 that God will *"render to each one according to his deeds*: eternal life to those who by patient continuance in doing good seek for glory, honor, and immortality; but to those who are self-seeking and do not obey the truth, but obey unrighteousness — indignation and wrath." Hebrews 10:27 also speaks of the fiery indignation that will devour His adversaries.

The great tribulation that is coming upon the sinful world will come from God. Why is this great tribulation coming? The Scriptures say that its purpose is threefold: (1) to test those who dwell upon the earth; meaning those who refused to receive Christ prior to the rapture (Revelation 3:10); (2) that God might vent His wrath upon the wicked (Revelation 15:7); and (3) to destroy those who destroy the earth (Revelation 11:18). Those who fall in one or all of these categories will experience the great tribulation period.

In the Old Testament the Lord spoke to Abraham and told him of the impending judgment on the cities of Sodom and Gomorrah. In response, Abraham challenged the fairness of God. He asked, "Suppose there were fifty righteous within the city; would You also destroy the place and not spare it for the fifty righteous that were in it? Far be it from You to do such a thing as this, to slay the righteous with the wicked, so that the righteous should be as the wicked; far be it from You! Shall not the Judge of all the earth do right?" (Genesis 18:24-25). The Lord responded that if He found fifty righteous people He would spare the city for their sake.

Notice the whole premise of Abraham's intercession with God was that if judgment proceeds from God, it wouldn't be fair for God to judge the righteous with the wicked. Nowhere in the Scripture — when we find judgment proceeding directly from God — do we find the righteous being judged along with the wicked.

When the angels arrived in Sodom, they couldn't even find the ten righteous for whom Abraham had interceded. So, they delivered the one righteous man, Lot, out of the city. Not until he was delivered did the judgment of God come. They declared in Genesis 19:22 that they could not do anything until he was safely out of the way.

In Luke 17, Jesus points out that on the same day Lot was brought out of the city, the judgment of God fell. In 2 Peter 2:6 the apostle points out that the cities of Sodom and Gomorrah were destroyed, "making them an example." However, God delivered that righteous man, Lot, who was vexed by the way people were living around him. Then Peter adds, "The Lord knows how to deliver the godly out of temptations and to reserve the unjust under punishment for the day of judgment" (2 Peter 2:9).

We're told in 1 Thessalonians 5:9 that God has not appointed us to wrath. Also, in Romans 5:9 we're told that, "having now been justified by His blood, we shall be saved from wrath through Him."

Any argument that might be developed to prove that the church will go through the great tribulation and experience the coming wrath of God must somehow answer these questions: When did God change His ways? When did He decide He would punish the righteous along with the wicked? It would be a change in God's nature to force His children to face the outpouring of His wrath; yet, God declares in Malachi 3:6, "I am the LORD, I do not change."

In deductive logic, the most common form of reasoning is known as a syllogism. A syllogism consists of a major premise, a minor premise, and a conclusion. When one premise is negative and the other positive, only a negative conclusion can follow. For example, a major premise might be positive: all birds have wings. The minor premise is negative: dogs do not have wings. The conclusion must be negative: dogs are not birds.

Our major premise is negative: the church is not appointed to wrath (Greek: orge). The minor premise is positive: the great tribulation is a time of God's wrath (orge). "Fall on us and hide us from the face of Him who sits on the throne and from the wrath of the Lamb! For the great day of His wrath has come" (Revelation 6:16–17). The conclusion must be negative and plain: the church will not experience the great tribulation. To argue any differently is to defy logic, and one may as well seek to prove that a dog is a bird. No further argument is necessary to prove that the church will not go through the great tribulation (see Act II). The burden of evidence is overwhelming.

## SCENE 2: The 70 Weeks

Around 538 BC while the prophet Daniel was praying and waiting upon God, he realized that the seventy years of Babylonian captivity were nearly over. And suddenly, the angel Gabriel appeared to Daniel.

As I previously stated in Daniel 9:24 Gabriel declared that, "Seventy weeks are determined for your people and for your holy city, to finish the transgression, to make an end of sins, to make reconciliation for iniquity, to bring in everlasting righteousness, to seal up vision and prophecy, and to anoint the Most Holy."

The angel went on to say that from the time the commandment would go forth to restore and rebuild Jerusalem to the coming of the Messiah would be 7 sevens and 62 sevens, or a total of 69 sevens. Since each seven represents a 7-year period, 69 sevens would be 483 years. In his book, *The Coming Prince*,[7] Sir Robert Anderson explains that this period would have to be predicated on the Babylonian calendar of 360 days per year. Thus, 483 years would be 173,880 days. On March 14, 445 BC, King Artaxerxes of Persia gave the commandment to Nehemiah to restore and rebuild Jerusalem. 173,880 days later brings us to AD April 6, 32 — the date when Christ made His triumphant entry into the city of Jerusalem (according to Anderson's calculation).[8]

The first part of the prophecy given to Daniel was fulfilled literally to the day. But the angel went on to say that the Messiah "shall be cut off, but not for Himself," literally, ['without receiving anything

---

[7] *The Coming Prince* by Sir Robert Anderson (Kregel Publications, 1975).

[8] The days are calculated in the following manner: 445 BC to AD 32 is 476 years. Multiply these years according to the Julian calendar of 365 days per year. This amounts to 173,740 days. Add 116 days for the corrected number of leap years and the difference of 24 days between March 14th and April 6th (reckoning inclusively according to Jewish practice). Thus, the total amounts to 173,880 days.

for Himself']. "And the people of the prince who is to come shall destroy the city and the sanctuary" (Daniel 9:26). The destruction of the city referred to the attack upon Jerusalem under Titus in AD 70. Titus was the general of the Roman legions, but he wasn't the prince of the people. Nero was the prince who ordered the destruction, though he died before the ravaging of Jerusalem was completed.

The city of Jerusalem and the sanctuary of the people were destroyed as the angel declared, and the Jews were dispersed. Thus far, we see the marvelously accurate fulfillment of this prophecy in history. However, Gabriel said that 70 sevens were determined upon Israel. The Messiah was cut off after 69 sevens. Where then is the seventieth seven?

In Daniel 9:27 the angel speaks again about the prince, using the pronoun "he." "Then he shall confirm a covenant with many for one week." The 69 "weeks" were to last from the commandment to restore and rebuild Jerusalem to the coming of Jesus Christ.

As predicted, the Messiah was "cut off" without receiving the kingdom, and the Jews were dispersed. The seventieth and final "week" of Daniel is still in the future.

Jesus referred to this prophetic "week" in Matthew 24 when the disciples asked Him about the signs of His coming and the end of the age. In verses 15-17, He said, "Therefore when you see the 'abomination of desolation,' spoken of by Daniel the prophet, standing in the holy place" (whoever reads, let him understand), "then let those who are in Judea flee to the mountains. Let him who is on the housetop not go down to take anything out of his house."

Then Jesus predicted a time of "great tribulation" such as the world has never seen before or will ever see again. This abomination that triggers the desolation takes place in the middle of the seventieth seven.

Daniel speaks of this "abomination of desolation" in chapter 9. The prince of the people will "confirm a covenant with many for one week; but in the middle of the week He shall bring an end to sacrifice and offering. And on the wing of abominations shall be one who makes desolate, even until the consummation, which is determined, is poured out on the desolate" (Daniel 9:27).

Since Jesus referred to this final seven–year period as yet future in His day, and inasmuch as the Antichrist hasn't yet made the covenant with Israel, we must conclude that it's still in the future. The fact that the Antichrist makes the covenant for seven years indicates that it's signed at the beginning of the final seven–year period.

Halfway through the seven years, the Antichrist will break the covenant with Israel as he causes the daily sacrifices and offerings in the temple to cease. According to Daniel 12:11, from that precise day until the end will be 1,290 days. Then Jesus will return again with His church in the clouds with great glory, just as Paul said in Colossians 3:4, "When Christ who is our life appears, then you also will appear with Him in glory."

The church age fits between the sixty–ninth and seventieth week of Daniel's prophecy. According to Paul in Ephesians 3:5 this mystery was hidden from the Old Testament writers.

At the present time God has poured out His Spirit of grace upon the Gentiles, from whom He is drawing a bride for His Son. When the fullness of the Gentiles has come in, God will then catch up His church, the waiting bride. This is the rapture of the church.

## NOT EVEN THE GATES OF HELL

In chapter 13 of the book of Revelation, we read about the coming of the man of sin who makes "war with the saints." Verse 7 of chapter 13 tells us, "It was granted to him to make war with the saints and to overcome them."

Daniel also testified to this fact. In chapter 7, verse 21 he describes the "little horn," or the Antichrist. "I was watching; and the same horn was making war against the saints, and prevailing against them." However, Jesus said that the gates of hell wouldn't prevail against His church (Matthew 16:18). It's impossible that the saints of Revelation 13 and Daniel 7 could be in the church, because the Antichrist cannot triumph over the church.

As we discussed in Scene I of this chapter, a syllogism is a form of deductive reasoning. As explained, when you have a negative premise and a positive premise, you can only reach a negative conclusion. The major premise is that the gates of hell cannot prevail against the church. The minor premise is that the saints are overcome by the Antichrist. And the obvious conclusion is that the saints are not the church. The saints must then be Israel, which are also the "elect" of Matthew 24:31.

## SCENE 3: The Restraining Force

In 2 Thessalonians 2, Paul wrote to correct an error that had crept into the church. Some false teachers were saying that the day of the Lord had already come. Paul told the Thessalonians that "that day," the second coming of Jesus Christ to reign over the earth, wouldn't take place until there was first a falling away, or departure, and the man of sin, the son of perdition, was revealed. Paul reminded the believers that he had told them these things when he was with them.

In chapter 2 Paul declared, "And now you know what is restraining, that he may be revealed in his own time. For the mystery of lawlessness is already at work; only He who now restrains will do so until He is taken out of the way. And then the lawless one will be revealed, whom the Lord will consume with the breath of His mouth and destroy with the brightness of His coming" (2 Thessalonians 2:6-8).

What is the "restraining" force holding back the revelation of the Antichrist? I believe it is the power of the Holy Spirit working in and through the church. As long as the Spirit-filled church is upon the earth, the unveiling of the Antichrist will be held back. As soon as the church is removed, nothing will stand in the way of the Antichrist. He'll be free then to take over the governments of the world.

The Holy Spirit will not be removed from the world, for He is omnipresent. However, during this time He will be working with Israel. Ezekiel 39:29 says that God will put His Spirit upon the nation Israel at the time the Russian army is destroyed. This event will possibly mark the beginning of the final seven–year period determined upon Israel.

I see the whole picture coming together very beautifully. After the church is removed, the Antichrist will be revealed. In Revelation 6, the first event that takes place when the seven–sealed scroll is opened is the white horse coming forth with his rider. This apparently is the Antichrist coming upon the earth. Since the church has been removed and is now rejoicing with the Lord in heaven, nothing restrains this wicked one from moving forward and taking over the world.

## SCENE 4: The Trumpets

Those who teach that the church must go through the great tribulation and face the coming wrath of God try to identify the last trump of 1 Corinthians 15 with the seventh trumpet in the book of Revelation. I see great difficulties in paralleling these two trumpets.

First of all, the trumpet that sounds at the time of the rapture of the church in 1 Thessalonians 4:16 is called the "trump of God." In Revelation, the seventh trumpet is the trumpet of the seventh angel.

The trump of 1 Corinthians 15 is used to proclaim an event that happens "in a moment, in the twinkling of an eye, at the last trumpet" (15:52). On the other hand, the seventh trump of the book of Revelation will cover a period of days. Revelation 10:7 says, "But in the days [plural] of the sounding of the seventh angel, when he is about to sound, the mystery of God would be finished, as He declared to His servants the prophets."

The last trump of 1 Corinthians 15 and 1 Thessalonians 4 will be a trumpet of glory. We shall be changed and made into His image and caught up to meet the Lord in the air. However, the seventh trumpet of the book of Revelation is continually referred to as a woe.

In Revelation 8:13 the angel said, "Woe, woe, woe, to the inhabitants of the earth, because of the remaining blasts of the trumpet of the three angels who are about to sound!" The angel says this at the end of the fourth trumpet. So, the three "woes" refer to the fifth, sixth, and seventh trumpets. At the end of the fifth trumpet (Revelation 9:12), the angel declares, "One woe is past. Behold, still two more woes are coming after these things." This refers to the sixth and seventh trumpets.

In Revelation 11:14 the angel declares, "The second woe is past. Behold, the third woe is coming quickly." Then we go right into verse 15, the seventh trumpet, which is actually the third woe.

Being raptured and changed into His glorious likeness is far from a woe. It would only be a woe if I didn't go! Thus, I see great difficulty in identifying the seventh trumpet of Revelation 11 and the last trumpet of 1 Corinthians 15 as one and the same, because the results and the time factors are so different.

In his New Testament Greek commentary on 1 Corinthians 15:52, Dean Henry Alford declares that no reason exists to define the last trump to be the seventh trumpet of Revelation.[9] He also says that there's no reason to assume that there aren't any trumpets after the last trump of 1 Corinthians 15.

## SCENE 5: The First Resurrection

Another major argument used by those who teach that the church will go through the great tribulation centers around Revelation 20:4–5. John said, "And I saw thrones, and they sat on them, and judgment was committed

---

[9] Henry Alford, Alford's Greek Testament (Grand Rapids: Guardian Press).

to them. Then I saw the souls of those who had been beheaded for their witness to Jesus and for the word of God, who had not worshiped the beast or his image, and had not received his mark on their foreheads or on their hands. And they lived and reigned with Christ for a thousand years. But the rest of the dead did not live again until the thousand years were finished. This is the first resurrection."

The argument presented is that "the first resurrection" means there was no resurrection prior to it. First means first, and nothing could be before it. However, if you try to make the first resurrection all take place in Revelation 20, after Satan is bound and cast into the abusso for a thousand years, you must somehow explain why Jesus was called the "firstfruits of those who rise from the dead." Did not Jesus already rise?

Also, there's a great multitude in heaven in Revelation 7:10 crying, "Salvation belongs to our God who sits on the throne, and to the Lamb!" When the elder asked John, "Who are these arrayed in white robes, and where did they come from?" (7:13). John answered that he didn't know. The elder responded, "These are the ones who come out of the great tribulation, and washed their robes and made them white in the blood of the Lamb. Therefore they are before the throne of God, and serve

Him day and night in His temple" (Revelation 7:14-15). Here in chapter 7 is a multitude in heaven who have come out of the great tribulation, thus resurrected before Revelation 20.

In Revelation 15 we see another company in heaven. John describes the sea of glass mingled with fire, and he sees those who had gained victory over the beast, over his image, over his mark, and over the number of his name. These people are standing on the sea of glass with the harps of God. They're singing the song of Moses, the servant of God. So, these would be the redeemed of Israel who had gained victory over the beast. John sees them in heaven before the seven final vials of God's wrath are poured out.

Here are two resurrected companies in heaven who have had a part in the first resurrection — prior to Revelation 20, when John sees those who had been beheaded for their witness of Jesus and refers to the "first resurrection."

In Revelation 20:4, John sees two distinctly different companies. First of all, he sees thrones and those who sat upon them. Judgment was given to them. No doubt, this is the church. The Lord made a promise to those who would overcome in the church of Laodicea. He promised to grant to them that they should sit with Him in His throne, even as He also overcame and has sat down with His Father on His throne (Revelation 3:21). Then John sees a second company in Revelation 20:4. These are the souls of those who were beheaded for the witness of Jesus, who hadn't worshiped the beast or his image, neither had they received his mark on their foreheads. These are two definite, separate companies. One is sitting upon thrones; the other came up out of the great tribulation, having been delivered from the power of the Antichrist and not yielding to his rule.

The first resurrection takes place over a period of time. Those who advocate that the church will go through this time of God's wrath say that the first resurrection is the resurrection of the last day. They insist on a literal twenty-four hour day. The first resurrection actually covers a period of time and encompasses many different events. There are those who rose when Jesus rose from the dead (Matthew 27:52); those coming back with Christ when He comes to catch us away to meet Him in the air (1 Thessalonians 4:14); and those who are martyred for their testimony of Jesus Christ and who will rise during the period of the great tribulation. These all have a part in the first resurrection. The first resurrection exists in contradistinction to the second resurrection, the resurrection of the unjust to stand before the great white throne judgment of God.

## SCENE 6: Watch & Be Ready

It's obvious that Jesus intended His disciples and the church in each age to anticipate His return at any time for them. His word to the disciples was to watch and be ready; for they wouldn't know the day nor the hour when He was coming, and He was coming at a time when they wouldn't expect. Therefore, they should always be watching and ready.

If you argue that the church must go through the great tribulation, then you're taking away from the imminent return of Jesus Christ. The church will not be watching, nor do we have any need to be watching for His return, if we must first go through the great tribulation. In that case, we'd be watching for the great tribulation or the unveiling of the Antichrist. The church could actually follow the final events rather carefully.

The first major event would be the unveiling of the Antichrist, when he would establish His reign and institute his new monetary system. Christians would then have to devise some way to survive without buying or selling. Next, we would watch for the great judgments predicted to come upon the earth. We would be especially watching for the Antichrist to stand in the Holy of Holies of the rebuilt temple, proclaim himself to be

God, and stop the daily sacrifices and prayers. According to Daniel, we know from that point that the Lord would be returning in 1,290 days (Daniel 12:11).

The Bible says that no man knows the day nor the hour (Matthew 24:36). This cannot refer to the day Christ returns to reign on earth, because that exact day has been given to us in Daniel's prophecy. No man knows the day or the hour when the Lord will take His church out of the earth. Therefore, we must be watching — not for the tribulation or the unveiling of the Antichrist — but for Jesus Christ to come for us at any time!

In Matthew 24:42 Jesus begins His exhortations to watch and be ready by giving a series of parables.

The first is an allegory concerning the master of the house. If the man had only known in what hour the thief was going to come, he would have watched and wouldn't have allowed his house to be broken into. "Therefore," Jesus said, "you also be ready, for the Son of Man is coming at an hour you do not expect" (Matthew 24:44).

Then Jesus gave the parable of the faithful and wise servant, who had been made ruler over the household. When his master returns, and finds him doing good, he will make him ruler over all his goods (24:45-47).

Jesus warned about the evil servant who would say in his heart, "My lord delays his coming." I believe that any time you teach that the rapture cannot take place until after the tribulation or after the revelation of the Antichrist, you're saying in effect that the Lord is delaying His coming, at least until the unveiling of the Antichrist or the great tribulation is over.

Jesus exhorts us that such a belief led to slothfulness by the servant. The lord came in an hour when the servant wasn't expecting him. The servant then was given his portion with the unbelievers. In contrast, believing that the Lord could come at any moment tends toward diligence and purity. In 1 John 3:2 we are told that "now we are children of God; and it has not yet been revealed what we shall be, but we know that when He is revealed, we shall be like Him, for we shall see Him as He is." We are then told that "everyone who has this hope in Him purifies himself, just as He is pure" (1 John 3:3). It is clear that the Lord wants us to be watching and ready for His coming — not watching for the tribulation or its beginning, or for the Antichrist or his revelation.

Be watching for Jesus Christ to come for us at any moment. To put any event before the coming of Christ for His church is, in essence, saying that the Lord will delay His coming until after that event has happened. Teaching or believing this is very dangerous, as Jesus Himself warned.

Through Matthew 25 Jesus emphasizes the necessity of being ready. In the parable of the ten virgins, the five foolish virgins weren't ready for the Lord when He came. When the cry went forth, "Behold, the bridegroom is coming," those who were ready went in. In verse 13 Jesus said, "Watch therefore, for you know neither the day nor the hour in which the Son of Man is coming."

We firmly believe that the coming of Christ is imminent; that not one single tribulation prophecy will be fulfilled before He catches up His church, and that He has intended the church of every generation to be watching and waiting for His return. In Mark 13:35-37 Jesus said, "Watch therefore, for you do not know when the master of the house is coming — in the evening, at midnight, at the crowing of the rooster, or in the morning — lest, coming suddenly, he find you sleeping. And what I say to you, I say to all: Watch!"

## SCENE 7: The Time Of The End

The Lord has given us some special promises relating to the great tribulation and the church. The first promise is in Revelation 3:10, where He told His faithful church of Philadelphia, "Because you have kept My command to persevere, I also will keep you from the hour of trial which shall come upon the whole world, to test those who dwell on the earth." Interpreting this verse to mean that Jesus would keep us in the tribulation and take us through it by divine preservation is totally without solid scriptural foundation and lacks sound scholarship. Such an interpretation is reading into a Scripture something that isn't there in order to harmonize it with a presupposition. Nowhere does the book of Revelation speak about any divine preservation for the church. The only divine preservation is for 144,000 Israelites who are sealed and, thus, spared from a portion of the judgments to come. Chapter 12 speaks also of this, where the woman is given wings of an eagle to bear her into the wilderness to escape from the wrath of the dragon for three-and-a-half years.

In 1 Thessalonians 5:9 Paul wrote about the coming of Christ for His church. "For God did not appoint us to wrath, but to obtain salvation through our Lord Jesus Christ." It's absolutely inconsistent with the nature of God to think that after Jesus bore completely the judgment for my sins, God would have me judged with the wicked world. God's wrath and judgment will be poured out upon a Christ-rejecting world. As a child of God, why would God number me with the unrighteous? God has not appointed us unto wrath.

Another interesting promise is found in Isaiah 26:19–21. The Lord first speaks of the resurrection of the dead. Then He says, "Come, my people, enter your chambers, and shut your doors behind you; hide yourself, as it were, for a little moment, until the indignation is passed. For, behold, the LORD comes out of His place to punish the inhabitants of the earth for their iniquity; the earth will also disclose her blood, and will no more cover her slain."

Isaiah is prophesying of the day when the Lord comes to punish the inhabitants of the earth — the great tribulation period. But God invites His people to enter into His chambers and shut the doors about them, so they might be hid for a moment until the indignation (the tribulation) is over.

This could refer to the Jews who will flee to the rock city of Petra and be preserved from the great tribulation. Isaiah also mentions this in chapter 16. "Let My outcasts dwell with you, O Moab; be a shelter to them from the face of the spoiler. For the extortioner is at an end, devastation ceases, the oppressors are consumed out of the land. In mercy the throne will be established; and One will sit on it in truth, in the tabernacle of David, judging and seeking justice and hastening righteousness" (Isaiah 16:4-5).

In this text, the people of Moab are told to take the Jews and shelter them in Sela, which is Petra, during the time when the Antichrist will try to destroy the Jews. Why would the Lord shield the Jews and not the church from the great tribulation?

And if the Lord has a separate plan to shield the church from the great tribulation, then where are those promises? Where does the Bible show the church as being sealed, protected, or marked, so that it wouldn't be harmed during the great tribulation? As John clearly details all the specific events of the last days in the book of Revelation, what passages tell of the church's preservation in the tribulation?

In Luke 21:34-36, Jesus talks about the great tribulation and His coming again. He tells us, "Take heed to yourselves, lest your hearts be weighed down with carousing, drunkenness, and cares of this life, and that Day come on you unexpectedly. For it will come as a snare on all those who dwell on the face of the whole earth. Watch therefore, and pray always that you may be counted worthy to escape all these things that will come to pass, and to stand before the Son of Man."

Escape all *what* things that shall come to pass? Surely I don't want to escape the Lord's coming for His church. That wouldn't make sense. No, Jesus was referring to the great tribulation that is coming, and I'd surely like to escape that! So I'm praying and watching just as Jesus told me to do.

I expect to be among those standing before the throne of God in the great multitude of Revelation 5, when Jesus takes the scroll out of the right hand of Him who is sitting upon the throne. I don't expect to be on earth when the seals are opened and God begins to pour out His wrath and indignation upon this godless, Christ-rejecting world. This makes the coming of Christ a blessed hope for the believers. We're passionately looking for that blessed hope, the glorious appearing of our great God and Savior, Jesus Christ.

The Old Testament tells us of two times when the earth was judged by God: the flood of Noah's day and the fire and brimstone that destroyed Sodom at the time of Lot. Jesus likened both of these analogies to the time of His return. "But as the days of Noah were, so also will the coming of the Son of Man be" (Matthew 24:37).

In Luke 17:28-29 we're told, "It was the same in the days of Lot. People were eating and drinking, buying and selling, planting and building. But the day Lot left Sodom, fire and sulfur rained down from heaven and destroyed them all." In both cases the righteous were delivered before the judgment of God came.

Noah was a type of the 144,000 sealed by God, so to speak, in the ark and protected in the judgment; Lot is a type of the church delivered from the judgment. We also have the case of the three Hebrew children in Daniel who were protected in the fiery furnace. The question is, "Where was Daniel?" Do you think he bowed to Nebuchadnezzar's image?

I think not. He is mysteriously away. Many believe that the image of Nebuchadnezzar was a type of the image of the beast in Revelation 13; the three Hebrew children the type of faithful Israel protected *in* the tribulation; and Daniel a type of the church protected *from* the tribulation.

One word should be said concerning the argument that the rapture isn't a traditional, historic church doctrine. While it's true that the anticipation of the Lord's return waned during much of church history, particularly during the Dark Ages, it's also true that the early church (of the

New Testament period) is part of the historic church. And Scripture clearly indicates that the early church was looking for the imminent return of Jesus Christ. Those Christians expected Him to come at any time for them. Remember that in 1 Thessalonians 4 the believers were sorrowing over their loved ones who had died before the Lord returned, thinking they were going to miss the kingdom age.

Moreover, there are many things in historic church doctrine with which I don't agree. Historic church doctrine teaches baptismal regeneration of infants. I don't believe that the Bible teaches baptismal regeneration of infants. The historic church teaches the intercession of Mary and the dead saints. I don't believe that the Bible teaches the intercession of the dead saints or Mary. The historic church teaches the infallibility of the pope. I don't believe in the infallibility of the pope.

Some historic church doctrine is unscriptural, in my opinion. I don't look at historic church doctrine as correct in every form and concept, nor do I see the historic church as a model for us to practice or follow. The only true model is found in the book of Acts. By the time John wrote the book of Revelation, so much false doctrine had crept in, that over and over Jesus called for the church to repent (Revelation 2 and 3).

Some claim that the interest in the rapture and its teachings grew out of the Plymouth Brethren in the late 1820s. The story goes that in a meeting in England a woman began to exhort the church through the gift of prophecy, and she said that the Lord was going to take His church out and save it from the wrath to come. We're told that men like John Nelson Darby and Cyrus I. Scofield then began to popularize this view.

In Daniel 12:4, the prophet sought an understanding from God as to the time of the end. The Lord told Daniel to "shut up the words, and seal the book until the time of the end; many shall run to and fro, and knowledge shall increase." In the context of this passage, increased knowledge is the knowledge of the prophetic truth that had been sealed until the time of the end.

As we approach the day in which the Lord takes His church out of this world, it would only be fitting that He make us more aware of the promise to the church of being caught up before the great tribulation. Why would the Lord reveal it to Martin Luther, John Calvin, or any Reformation church leaders? They weren't living in the age when the church was to be taken out.

The book of Daniel was to be sealed until the time of the end, and we're now in that time. Daniel 12:4

clearly promises that the knowledge of prophecy will be increased. Knowing that, we can safely assume that God will give us new insights into the understanding of His promises and His Word in these last days.

## ANTICHRIST ABOMINATIONS

- Daniel 9:27; 12:11
- Matthew 24:15
- 2 Thessalonians 2:4
- Revelation 11:2

## ANTICHRIST DICTATORSHIP, MANIFESTATION

- Revelation 13

## ANTICHRIST'S 7-YEAR COVENANT WITH ISRAEL

- Isaiah 28:18
- Daniel 9:27

## BABYLON ECONOMIC AND POLITICAL DESTRUCTION

- Revelation 18

## BATTLE OF ARMAGEDDON

- Psalm 2:1-5, 9
- Isaiah 34:1-6; 63:3-4, 6
- Joel 3:2, 9-16
- Zechariah 12:2; 14:2-3, 12
- Revelation 14:14-20; 16:16; 19:11-21

## CHURCH HARLOT (FALSE CHURCH)

- 1 Timothy 4:1-3
- 2 Timothy 3:1-5
- Revelation 17

## DARKNESS AND UTTER DEPRESSION

- Joel 2:2
- Revelation 16:10

## DAY OF THE LORD

- Isaiah 2:12; 13:6, 9
- Ezekiel 13:5; 30:3
- Joel 1:15; 2:1, 11, 31; 3:14
- Amos 5:18, 20
- Obadiah 15
- Zephaniah 1:7, 14
- Zechariah 14:1
- Malachi 4:5
- Acts 2: 20
- 1 Thessalonians 5:2
- 2 Thessalonians 2:2
- 2 Peter 3:10

## DEMONIC INVASIONS

- Revelation 9:3-20

## DEVIL WORSHIP AND IDOLATRY

- Revelation 9:20; 13:11-17

## DRUNKENNESS, DRUGS, AND ILLICIT SEX

- Matthew 24:38
- Luke 17:27
- Revelation 9:21

## FALSE MESSIAHS AND PROPHETS

- Matthew 24:5, 11-24

## FAMINE OF GOD'S WORD

- Amos 8:11-12

## FIRES AND SCORCHING SOLAR HEAT

- Revelation 16:8-9
- Revelation 18:8-9, 18

## GENTILES' PUNISHMENT

- Romans 1:18
- 2 Thessalonians 2:11-12
- Revelation 19:15

## GOD'S INDIGNATION

- Isaiah 26:20; 34:2
- Revelation 6:17

## GOD'S VENGEANCE

- Isaiah 34:8; 63:1-6

## GOG AND MAGOG INVADE ISRAEL

- Ezekiel 38-39

## GREAT TRIBULATION

- Matthew 24:21

## HARVEST BY GOD AND SATAN

- Matthew 13

## HOUR OF GOD'S JUDGMENT

- Revelation 14:7

## ISRAEL: DESTRUCTION ATTEMPT ON ISRAEL

- Revelation 12

## ISRAEL'S PURGE

- Ezekiel 20:23, 38
- Zechariah 13:8-9
- Malachi 3:3

## JEWS RETURN TO ISRAEL

- Isaiah 43:5-6
- Ezekiel 34:11-13; 36:24; 37:1-14

## MARTYRED MULTITUDE IN HEAVEN

- Revelation 7:9, 14

## MATERIALISM IN THE LAST DAYS

- Luke 17:28
- Revelation 18:12-14

## MULTITUDE FOR THE MILLENNIUM

- Matthew 25:32-34

## NO ESCAPE FROM GOD'S FIERCE JUDGMENT

- Amos 9:2-3

## PEOPLE FEARING GOD

- Isaiah 2:19-21
- Revelation 6:15-17

## PERSECUTION OF BELIEVERS

- Matthew 24:10
- Revelation 16:6; 17:6

## PERSECUTION OF ISRAEL

- Daniel 12:1
- Zechariah 11:16
- Matthew 24:21
- Revelation 12:13

## PLAGUES

- Zechariah 14:12
- Revelation 16:2

## PREPARATION FOR MILLENNIUM

- Revelation 16:20

## ROMAN EMPIRE REVIVAL

- Daniel 2:41; 7:7
- Revelation 13:1; 17:12

## SATAN CAST FROM HEAVEN

- Revelation 12:3-15

## SATAN'S LIE

- Isaiah 14:12-15

## SEVEN VIALS OF JUDGMENT

- Revelation 16

## SEVENTIETH WEEK

- Daniel 9:24-27

## SIGNS OF THE HEAVENS, STARS, MOON, AND SUN

- Isaiah 13:10, 13; 24:1, 19-20; 34:10
- Joel 2:10, 30-31; 3:15
- Revelation 6:12-14
- Revelation 8:7-11, 16:21

## SIX SEALS' JUDGMENT

- Matthew 24:4-8
- Revelation 6
- Revelation 8-9; 11:15-19

## SORROWS OF DEATH

- Isaiah 13:8
- Jeremiah 30:6
- Revelation 6:8

## THREE ANGELS' MESSAGE

- Revelation 14:6-12

## TIME OF JACOB'S TROUBLE

- Jeremiah 30:7

## TIME OF THE END

- Daniel 12:9
- Matthew 13:40, 49

## TRIBES OF ISRAEL CALLED, CONVERTED, MARTYRED

- Matthew 24:14
- Revelation 7:1-4
- Revelation 14:1-5

## TRIBULATION DEATHS

- Zephaniah 1:17
- Isaiah 34:3; 66:24
- Matthew 24:28
- Revelation 14:20
- Revelation 19:17-19

## TRIBULATION SURVIVORS

- Isaiah 13:12

## TWO WITNESSES

- Revelation 11:3-13

## WARS, FAMINES, EARTHQUAKES, DISASTERS

- Matthew 24:6-7
- Luke 21:25

- Revelation 6:2-6, 8
- Revelation 9:1-2; 14:20
- Revelation 6:12; 11-13; 16-18
- Revelation 8:7-12; 16:3

## WORLD RELIGION, POLITICS, AND ECONOMY

- Revelation 13:4-8, 16-17
- Revelation 17:1-18; 18:1-24

## WORLD TIME OF TROUBLE

- Daniel 12:1
- Matthew 24:21-22

ACT IV

# THE SECOND
# COMING

IN ACT III WE READ of the turmoil and tribulation of the world. But as stark as that scene was, it was only a warm-up to the drama about to unfold in Act IV. Against the dark backdrop of the great tribulation, Christ's second coming will reveal His majesty to a wide-eyed, gaping world.

The second coming of Jesus Christ occurs at the end of the great tribulation. It is during this time that Jesus will set up His rule on earth for a thousand-year period known as the millennium. However, the drama does not end there. At the end of this millennium period, Satan and his army will rise up in one final battle against Jesus. Only at the conclusion of that battle will we see the demise of Satan, and the judgment of the great white throne.

## SCENE 1: You See These Stones?

In chapters 23 and 24 of the Gospel of Matthew, the apostle describes a time when Jesus was in the temple castigating the Pharisees and disputing with them. As He and the disciples left the temple, the disciples started to comment on the huge stones that Herod had used in the rebuilding of the temple. And in relation to these mammoth stones, "huge" is almost an understatement. The smallest stones in the temple weighed a mere 2 to 3 tons — about the weight of an elephant. Many weighed 50 tons. And the largest existing stone — which you can see in the Rabbi's Tunnel in Jerusalem today — has been estimated to weigh a whopping 570 tons![10] As the disciples commented on those huge stones, Jesus said something alarming. He said, gesturing to the stones, "Assuredly, I say to you, not one stone shall be left here upon another" (Matthew 24:2).

I'm sure the disciples were perplexed. What could Jesus mean? Who could possibly move even one of those enormous stones? As they continued walking through the Kidron Valley and up the Mount of Olives, the disciples asked, "Tell us, when will these things be?" (24:3). They wanted to know what signs they should watch for — signs that would precede the destruction of the

---

[10] http://info.jpost.com/2000/Supplements/Millennium/tour1.html

temple. But they also wanted to know about the end of the world. "And what will be the sign of Your coming, and of the end of the age?" (Matthew 24:3).

## THE END OF THE WORLD AGE

People sometimes wonder why Christians are always talking about the end of the world. The truth is we're usually not talking about the end of the world, but the end of the world age. The end of the world is somewhere off in the distance. But the end of the world system, the end of man's feeble and futile attempt to try to rule over his fellowman without corruption, is what most Christians refer to when they say, "the end." Now the question is, when will the world age come to an end? What will be the signs of it? In Act I, we covered some of Jesus' specific answers to those questions. Jesus also gave a series of parables that would indicate that His second coming was close, and that the end of this world age was coming to an end.

Jesus promised that He would come again. He said to His disciples, "Let not your heart be troubled; you believe in God, believe also in Me. In My Father's house are many mansions; if it were not so, I would have told you. I go to prepare a place for you. And if I go and prepare a place for you, I will come again and receive you to Myself; that where I am, there you may be also"

(John 14:1-3). In this passage, Jesus is referring to His coming *for* the church, what is known as the rapture of the church (see Act II).

But Jesus is also coming one day *with* His church, back to establish the kingdom of God on earth.

## SCENE 2: The Second Coming of Jesus

The Bible is full of promises and prophecies concerning the second coming of Jesus. Both Old Testament and New Testament verses talk about that time when Jesus will establish God's kingdom here on earth. One such Old Testament verse is found in Daniel 7:13-14 where the prophet said, "I was watching in the night visions, and behold, One like the Son of Man, coming with the clouds of heaven! He came to the Ancient of Days, and they brought Him near before Him. Then to Him was given dominion and glory and a kingdom, that all peoples, nations, and languages should serve Him. His dominion is an everlasting dominion, which shall not pass away, and His kingdom the one which shall not be destroyed."

Zechariah also prophesied of the coming of Jesus. "And I will pour on the house of David and on the inhabitants of Jerusalem the Spirit of grace and supplication; then they will look on Me whom they pierced. Yes, they will mourn for Him as one mourns for his only son, and grieve for Him as one grieves for a firstborn" (Zechariah 12:10). Zechariah is telling us that when Jesus comes again, the Jews will then acknowledge and recognize that He is the Messiah. They will look upon Him whom they had pierced and they will mourn over the fact that they were blind for so many years to the true Messiah that God had sent to their fathers—the Messiah who had been rejected just as prophesied: "He is despised and rejected by men, a Man of sorrows and acquainted with grief" (Isaiah 53:3).

A similar verse in Revelation 1:7 declares, "Behold, He is coming with clouds, and every eye will see Him, even they who pierced Him. And all the tribes of the earth will mourn because of Him. Even so, Amen."

In Matthew 24:30, Jesus said, "Then the sign of the Son of Man will appear in heaven, and then all the tribes of the earth will mourn, and they will see the Son of Man coming on the clouds of heaven with power and great glory." The last time the disciples saw Jesus before He ascended into heaven from the Mount of Olives is recorded in Acts 1:9-11, which reads, "Now when He had spoken these things, while they watched, He was taken up, and a cloud received Him out of their sight.

And while they looked steadfastly toward heaven as He went up, behold, two men stood by them in white apparel, who also said, "Men of Galilee, why do you stand gazing up into heaven? This same Jesus, who was taken up from you into heaven, will so come in like manner as you saw Him go into heaven."

Again, back in Zechariah 14:4, he tells us that when He comes again, "And in that day His feet will stand on the Mount of Olives, which faces Jerusalem on the east. And the Mount of Olives shall be split in two, from east to west, making a very large valley; half of the mountain shall move toward the north and half of it toward the south." In Colossians 3:4, Paul said, "When Christ *who is* our life appears, then you also will appear with Him in glory." Jude 1:14 quotes from the prophecy of Enoch and wrote, "Now Enoch, the seventh from Adam, prophesied about these men also, saying, 'Behold, the Lord comes with ten thousands of His saints.'" In Revelation 19:11-15, in talking about the coming again of Jesus, John said, "Now I saw heaven opened, and behold, a white horse. And He who sat on him was called Faithful and True, and in righteousness He judges and makes war. His eyes were like a flame of fire, and on His head were many crowns. He had a name written that no one knew except Himself. He was clothed with a robe dipped in blood, and His name is called The Word of God. And the armies in heaven, clothed in fine linen, white and clean, followed Him on white horses. Now out of His mouth goes a sharp sword, that with it He should strike the nations. And He Himself will rule them with a rod of iron. He Himself treads the winepress of the fierceness and wrath of Almighty God."

## DETAILS OF CHRIST'S COMING

So the prophecies concerning the second coming of Jesus Christ are abundant throughout Scriptures. What do these prophecies tell us about the second coming?

First, Jesus will be coming in the clouds of heaven.

Secondly, the whole world shall see Him.

Third, the Jews will recognize Jesus and "look upon Him whom they had pierced."

Fourth, the saints will return with Him. Those who have been taken up in the rapture will accompany Him as He comes to establish the kingdom of God upon the earth. "When Christ *who is* our life appears, then you also will appear with Him in glory" (Colossians 3:4).

Fifth, just as He ascended from the Mount of Olives, He will descend upon the Mount of Olives. When His foot touches there, the Mount of Olives will cleave right there in the center, a new valley will be formed, and part of the mountain will move toward the north and part of it toward the south.

## TIMING

What is the timing of His coming again? As we discussed in Act II and Act III, two events will precede Christ's second coming — the rapture and the tribulation. Now, there is a possibility that one other prophecy will be fulfilled before the rapture of the church. That other potential sign is the invasion of Israel by Islamic nations that will attempt to destroy Israel and wipe it from the face of the earth.

The Bible predicts that this will happen in the last days. According to Scripture, Russia will support these Islamic nations as they invade Israel (see Act I). The Bible tells us that ultimately, the Muslims will attempt a war of extermination against Israel.

This war will be interrupted by God's intervention. Right when it looks totally impossible for Israel, when it looks like there is no way that they can possibly survive, God will intervene and destroy five-sixths of this invading army. God will manifest His power in such a way that Israel will know that it was only His intervention that saved them.

Following the defeat of these Islamic nations (and the Russian forces backing them), an extremely powerful, extremely gifted man will rise to lead the European Community. He will have tremendous charisma and he will be hailed by the world as its savior because he will seem to have answers that no one has been able to come up with: answers to the identity crisis, answers to the crime problem, answers to the Middle East hostilities between the Arabs and the Jews.

## 1,290 DAYS

Sometime during this period when Russia supports the Muslims in their invasion of Israel, the Lord will rapture His church out of the earth and put His Spirit upon the nation of Israel. Now will begin the final seven-year period during which God will deal with His people Israel.

During this time, the Jews will rebuild their temple in Jerusalem. They will institute again the daily prayers and sacrifices. It is interesting that the Jews have already prepared the priests' robes and many of the articles that will be used in the temple worship, and they are making preparations for the rebuilding of the temple, even though at this point they don't know how it could possibly happen.

But after a happy three-and-a-half years, this man — the leader of Europe — will come into the rebuilt temple in

Jerusalem and stop the daily prayers and sacrifices. Not only that, he will stand in the holy place, declare himself to be God, and demand to be worshiped as God. If you find yourself still here and you somehow manage to survive to this point, start marking your calendar from that day. Count one thousand two hundred and ninety days, and you'll know the exact day of Jesus' second coming. As previously discussed, this time frame was revealed to Daniel in chapter 12 of the book bearing his name. We read there that from the time the daily sacrifices are stopped unto the coming of the Messiah will be one thousand two hundred and ninety days.

Upon reading that last paragraph, some will argue, "You said no man knows the day or the hour of Christ's return." Remember: we can't confuse the rapture of the church with the second coming of Christ. The rapture could happen at any moment. It could happen before you finish reading this paragraph. We don't know the day or the hour of that event. But we do know that from the time the Antichrist stops the daily prayers and sacrifices in the temple, we can count forward one thousand two hundred and ninety days and we will know the exact date of the second coming of Jesus Christ. This sacrilege, this standing in the temple and declaring that he is God and demanding to be worshiped as God, will be what you might call the last straw. This act of blasphemy and defilement will bring an end to the patience of God and will usher in the great tribulation, as God's wrath and judgment are finally poured out upon this world in unbelievable and immeasurable force (see Act III).

## SCENE 3: The Millennium

Do you find yourself weary of this world, and the governments who attempt to rule it? If so, take heart. Life on earth will be different during the period known as the millennium. In this thousand-year period, earth will finally be ruled by One who reigns with righteousness. Jesus will establish His kingdom here on earth, and we — and all the saints who have lived before us — will reign with Him. Unlike today, when people ignore the laws they don't agree with or establish grass roots "rebellion" to try to undermine our laws, the rule of Christ will be ironclad. His word will be law.

Among the different structures of government the world has tried — socialism, communism, democracy, monarchy, etc. — the most efficient form of government is a monarchy. A monarchy can be a good system if the monarch is good, but it's awful if the monarch is a tyrant. Jesus, the King of Kings, will rule with a righteous rule and a righteous reign. Those who don't want to comply will be dealt with severely. As I understand it, we who come with Christ to reign in His new kingdom will be given authority over specific territories. We will be the enforcers of righteousness.

## WHAT WILL THE EARTH BE LIKE?

As we discussed in Acts II, Adam's sin in the Garden of Eden caused a change in ownership of the world. When he chose to rebel against God's command, Adam forfeited the title deed to earth. Satan took ownership, and the world has suffered from every moment since.

Jesus paid the redemption price for earth when He went to the cross. He purchased earth back for God. And at His second coming, He will return to claim that which He purchased through His death.

Several things will happen when Jesus takes back the title deed to earth. First, Satan will be bound for the duration of the millennium, meaning that we will not have to deal with him during that thousand-year period.

Then the earth will be restored to what it was before the flood, as it was in the Garden of Eden. The earth will be a paradise. There will likely be an equalizing of the climates, which means no more hurricanes, no more tornadoes. We know that at one time, forests existed under what are now polar icecaps. Coal deposits tell us that. And in the icy tundra of the frozen Arctic Circle in Siberia, the remains of mammoths have been found. When these beasts were cut open, their digestive tracts contained tropical vegetation. Those discoveries tell us that at one time, the climate of the earth was vastly different than it is today. The North Pole was populated by tropical animals, and not polar icecaps. Without the polar icecaps, more land surface would be covered by water, and the ratio of sea to land would change from what it is today. But without those polar icecaps, we would also not have such radical variances in climate.

Presently, the earth is tilted at twenty-three and a third degrees, which gives us our seasons. But it's possible that God will readjust this tilt, because the Bible says the earth is going to wobble like a drunken man and will be moved out of its place. Perhaps the Lord will correct the earth's tilt to where we're directly perpendicular to the sun, which would eliminate seasons and bring an equal kind of daylight and nighttime. If that happened, the whole earth might be like Hawaii. And with that, a renewed longevity of life.

More water in the oceans would mean more evaporation, which means greater moisture in the atmosphere. This increase in atmospheric moisture would mean greater filter protection from harmful ultraviolet rays.

In every way imaginable, earth will improve. The planet will be beautiful. The whole earth will be filled with His glory. Righteousness will cover the earth as the waters cover the seas. And we will be here, living and reigning with Christ, and enjoying the world as it was intended.

## WHEN JESUS RETURNS, WHAT WILL HE DO?

When Jesus returns to establish His kingdom, the first order of business will be to gather the nations together for judgment to determine which of those who survived the great tribulation will be allowed the privilege of living in the kingdom age.

Those who took the mark of the beast will not be allowed to enter into the kingdom age — in fact, they will immediately be eliminated. It is at that time that the Lord will separate the people as a shepherd separates the sheep from the goats. To those on His right hand, He'll say, "Then the King will say to those on His right hand, 'Come, you blessed of My Father, inherit the kingdom prepared for you from the foundation of the world'" (Matthew 25:34). But to those on His left, He'll say, "Then He will also say to those on the left hand, 'Depart from Me, you cursed, into the everlasting fire prepared for the Devil and his angel'" (25:41). Jesus will then begin the thousand-year reign, and we will reign with Him as a kingdom of priests over the earth. We are told that we will go annually to Jerusalem to meet with the Lord.

The millennium will bring not only a change in earth's climate, but a change within man himself. Sickness will be abolished. Handicaps will be abolished. Isaiah speaks of those glorious days when the lame will leap for joy, the mute will shout for joy, and the blind will behold the glory of the Lord. We will experience no more sorrow, no more pain, no more suffering.

People will be healed of their ailments, and they will be restrained from following their sin nature. During the thousand-year reign of Jesus Christ, people will have no choice but to live righteously. Within this ideal environment, there will be no opportunity to give vent to their evil desires. We'll be there to see to that. We'll be there with extraordinary powers in our glorified bodies. Righteousness will be enforced upon all men. And for that thousand years we will see just how wonderful it is when people live in righteousness. We will have no need of police departments, judicial systems, or prisons. People living righteously will experience the blessings and benefits of living in harmony with God.

You may recall the parable of the talents in Matthew chapter 25, where one fellow who had been entrusted with five talents came back with five more and said, "Lord, you delivered to me five talents; look, I have gained five more talents besides them" (Matthew 25:20). His master then said, "Well done, good and faithful servant; you were faithful over a few things, I will make you ruler over many things. Enter into the joy of your lord" (25:21).

This is the reality for the believer. As we have demonstrated our faithfulness on earth, Jesus will entrust us with responsibility in the millennial kingdom. We will assist Christ in His reign by serving as kings over the cities He entrusts to us. We're told in Zechariah 14 that those who live during this period will come annually to Jerusalem to worship Jesus and keep the Feast of Tabernacles. Isaiah 2 adds that when we come into His house and sit at His feet, Jesus will teach us His ways. "'Come, and let us go up to the mountain of the LORD, to the house of the God of Jacob; He will teach us His ways, and we shall walk in His paths.' For out of Zion shall go forth the law, and the word of the LORD from Jerusalem" (Isaiah 2:3). Think of those annual meetings in Jerusalem! Think of sitting at the feet of Jesus and learning directly from Him!

## THE DEAD AND UNSAVED

During this thousand-year reign, we (the church) will be in our glorified bodies. Those who lived through the great tribulation will be in their natural bodies, living in a perfect climate under perfect conditions. Imagine how healthy those people will be with no more disease, no sickness, and no weather calamities.

So what happens to the unsaved during the time when we are reigning with Christ? Scripture tells us that, "But the rest of the dead did not live again until the thousand years were finished. This is the first resurrection" (Revelation 20:5). The first resurrection covers a long period of time. It began with Jesus Christ, and it will end when the last of the martyred saints is brought into glory. But the rest of the dead will not live again until the thousand years are finished.

## SCENE 4: Satan's Final Rebellion

After one thousand years of peace and righteousness — a time when disease, sickness, war, strife and calamity have been banished from earth — you can practically hear the menacing change in our drama's soundtrack as we reach Revelation 20. Gone are the light, tranquil sounds of flute and guitar chords, playing quietly in the background. From somewhere just off-stage, eerie piano notes and the rumbling of a bass drum begin to herald the shift in scene. Our villain is about to make his reappearance.

## RELEASED

> Now when the thousand years have expired, Satan will be released from his prison ... (Revelation 20:7).

Note what the first half of that verse clearly states: Satan is released. He doesn't escape, nor is he sprung loose by one of his demonic cohorts. He is set free. And the one doing the releasing is God.

But why would the Lord let Satan loose again? Some would ask, "Since God already had Satan chained and put away in the abyss, why didn't He just keep him there? Why let him go? And if Satan's ultimate destiny is destruction, why didn't God just destroy him a long time ago and save us all the misery and suffering he has brought upon the earth?" The answer, of course, is that God is sovereign, and He has a sovereign plan for the earth and its inhabitants. Satan serves a divine purpose, and God will allow him temporary freedom in order that he might serve that divine purpose.

How could this be? How could people who have lived under ideal conditions, and under the perfect and righteous reign of Jesus Christ, ever be persuaded to rise up against Him? It will happen because rebellion lurks in the hearts of men, and God permits this last display of mutiny and disobedience so that for all time and eternity, men will know that the problem of sin dwelt within them. No one will be able to say, "Well, it was my environment that caused me to be evil." That argument will be shot down forever after the desperate wickedness of man's heart will be revealed through this last rebellion against Jesus. Even while accepting the blessings and benefits of living under the righteous reign of Christ, sin had still lurked in their hearts.

## LOVE'S TEST

You know, it's so easy for us to say, "I love You, Lord, with all my heart. You are first. I love You more than anyone or anything else." It costs nothing to say the words. But we often say them without real sincerity. When we avow our love for God, oftentimes God tests us as to the extent of how much we really do love Him. And sometimes, Satan is God's instrument in that testing.

Job illustrates this for us. When the sons of God presented themselves to God and Satan came along with them, God questioned Satan as to where he had been. Satan answered, "From going to and fro on the earth, and from walking back and forth on it" (Job 1:7).

He wasn't out on a prayer walk, mind you. He was out surveying people and seeing who he might trip up or accuse.

So God suggested that he take a look at Job. "Have you considered My servant, Job? He's a good man. He loves me and he hates evil."

Satan scoffed at that. "Sure he loves you. You've put a hedge around him and you won't let anyone get to him. You've blessed and prospered him. Anyone would serve You if You prospered them the way You have Job. He has no needs, no wants. But just take away that hedge for a minute. Let me at him. I can make him curse You."

And so, to prove that Job did indeed love Him, God allowed Satan to strip Job of his possessions. He put just one restriction on Satan — he couldn't touch Job's life.

Satan's belief about Job was that he was nothing but a mercenary; he served God only for the perks and profits God threw his way. Satan's attitude was, "Take away the perks, and Job won't serve You anymore." It's true that God gives His children many wonderful perks. But do we serve Him for those blessings and benefits? Or do we serve Him because we love Him with our whole hearts?

God allowed Satan to test his theory. When Job had been stripped of his family and his fortune, he lay on the ground and said, "Naked I came from my mother's womb, and naked shall I return there. The LORD gave, and the LORD has taken away; blessed be the name of the LORD" (Job 1:21). The next verse tells us that, "In all of these things, Job did not curse God nor charge God foolishly." He accepted whatever God brought into his life. Satan was used merely as an instrument to test and demonstrate the sincerity of Job's love for God.

Love that is forced is no love at all. Suppose I were to say to my son, "I'm going downtown to purchase a desk. When I get back, I'm going to need help getting it upstairs into my office. I want you to stay here in the yard until I get back so you can help me with that." And then suppose I took my son out back and chained him to a big tree in the backyard. I go and get my desk, come home, find him still chained to that tree, and then, when I've unlocked him and forced him to help me carry my new desk inside, I say, "My, I have such a wonderful, obedient son. I'm so proud of that boy — he stayed in the backyard the whole while I was gone." My neighbor might be watching out the window, thinking, "You should have heard him screaming and ranting about you while you were gone."

But if on the other hand, I say, "Son, I'm going to get a desk. I want you to stay in the yard while I'm gone. Don't leave. I want you here when I get back." And as I take off, I see my neighbor out watering his lawn and I say, "Mr. Jones, would you mind just sort of keeping an eye on my son? I'm sort of curious to know what happens when I'm not around. I told him to stay in the yard, and I'm just curious to see what he'll do."

So I go down and get the desk, and when I get home, I ask the neighbor, "How did it go?"

And he says, "Oh, Mr. Smith, you've got a fine son. You don't have to worry about him. He stayed in the yard the whole time while you were gone. Not only that, but when the kid from up the street came over and asked your son to go shoot some baskets with him, your son said, 'No, I can't go. Dad wants me to stay here in the yard. He wants me here when he gets back.' And the kid up the street persisted. 'Oh, come on, let's go. You can get back here before your dad does. He'll never know you're gone. Come on, let's go.' Your son said, 'No, Dad told me to stay here and I'm going to stay here until he gets back.' That neighbor kid didn't give up, though. 'Ah, come on, you're just chicken.' And your son popped him in the nose. The kid went home with a bloody nose. Mr. Smith, you've got a fine son."

*Then* I could be justly proud that my son obeyed me even though he had the opportunity and the freedom to do otherwise.

Do you see the need for our testing? God has asked certain things of us. And rather than tying us or chaining us, He leaves us free. Then Satan comes along and tries to tempt us towards disobedience. When I remain true to God in spite of the temptations, then God receives pleasure and glory in my obedience to Him, especially in light of the fact that the opportunity to do otherwise was there. God says, "Oh, I've got a fine son," just as He did concerning Job.

So that is why God will allow Satan another moment of freedom. Just as he tests our love and commitment to God now, so, too, he will use his freedom to test those who dwell on the earth at the end of the millennial period.

With apparently very little effort, Satan amasses an army and persuades them to gather around the righteous with the intent to destroy them. "They went up on the breadth of the earth and surrounded the camp of the saints and the beloved city" (Revelation 20:9a). But God squelches the rebellion almost before it begins. "And fire came down from God out of heaven and devoured them" (20:9b).

It's all over in a moment. It's such a brief, pathetic rebellion that it can't even rightly be called a battle. But it serves a purpose. It shows the desperate wickedness of man's heart and the absolute righteousness of God's judgment when He pours His wrath upon wicked men.

And what of Satan, the brains behind this operation? "The Devil, who deceived them, was cast into the lake of fire and brimstone where the beast and the False Prophet are. And they will be tormented day and night forever and ever" (Revelation 20:10).

## LAKE OF FIRE

In Scripture, the lake burning with fire is known as Gehenna. Gehenna is a valley just south of Jerusalem that is also known as the Valley of Hinnom. In times of apostasy, when the nation of Israel worshiped Baal and Molech, the people would build bonfires to those gods and throw their babies into the fire as an act of worship. They referred to this as "causing your children to pass through the fire." This was considered an act of worship, but it was also a convenient method of getting rid of unwanted babies. They didn't know how to perform abortions in those days, so they would wait until the child was born and then they'd throw them into the bonfires as worship for their god of pleasure.

Later, in the time of Christ, the Valley of Hinnom became the garbage dump for the city of Jerusalem. They burned garbage constantly. Day or night, you could look towards the Valley of Hinnom and see smoke rising from the garbage fires of Hinnom.

The name Gehenna, therefore, carries the connotation of constant, eternal burning. It is described as a lake of fire and brimstone.

Now, the first occupants of Gehenna will be the Antichrist and the False Prophet. They will be the only occupants of the burning lake for the first thousand years, because during that time Satan will be bound and hidden away in a bottomless pit called the abyss. After his brief and futile rebellion against God, Satan will join the Antichrist and the False Prophet in Gehenna. Note in Revelation 20:10 that it says he will go "where the beast and the False Prophet *are*." This does not say "where the beast and the False Prophet were consumed" or "were destroyed." It says, "where they *are*." Some groups have such a hard time grasping the terror of Gehenna that they teach instead the annihilation of the wicked. That's easier to live with, but it's not true. You won't find that teaching in the Scripture. Instead, Scripture says of the wicked, "He shall be tormented with fire and brimstone in the presence of the holy angels and in the presence of the Lamb. And the smoke of their torment ascends forever and ever; and they have no rest day or night" (Revelation 14:10b-11a).

## THE JUDGMENTS

Once Satan's brief rebellion is crushed, the Lord begins His great white throne judgments, as recorded in Revelation 20:11-15.

God keeps accurate, precise, and complete records. Everything you've ever done or thought has been recorded. It may be similar to the science of "sound." Scientists theorize that sound goes on and on, continuing forever. We know that sound travels at about 727 miles an hour. Scientists conjecture that all the sound that has ever been created just continues on; that everything that has been said is out there somewhere. And if you could only tune in on it, you could play back the sound of your parents ooh'ing and ahh'ing over you as they first saw you there in the crib.

Whether or not that theory is true, we know from Scripture that everything we've ever said, or thought, or done has been recorded by God. He knows it all and He's recorded it all in what is called the Book of Life. Based upon what is written there, when God opens the book, you will be judged according to those thoughts, words and actions.

The Bible mentions this Book of Life several times. It is interesting to me that half of those references speak of people being blotted out of the book. When Moses is interceding for his people and he asks God to forgive them, adding that if He won't, Moses would like his own name blotted out of the book (Exodus 32:32). The Lord tells Moses, "Whosoever has sinned against Me, I will blot him out of My book" (32:33). In Psalm 69:28, David, speaking for the Messiah, says, "Let them be blotted out of the book of the living and not written with the righteous."

Jesus, in His message to the church of Sardis in the third chapter of Revelation, promised that those who overcame would be clothed with white raiment and their names would not be blotted out of the book of life. Instead, Jesus promised, He would confess their names before God and His angels. And then in Revelation 22:19, we're warned that "If anyone takes away from the words of the book of this prophecy, God shall take away his part from the Book of Life, from the holy city, and from the things which are written in this book."

## THE SECOND DEATH

If you have a part in the first resurrection, you will never face the second death. From a scriptural definition, death is the separation of a man's consciousness from

God. If you live outside of a consciousness of God — if there is no place for God in your life, no communion, no fellowship, no thought of God — then according to the Scriptures, you are dead already. Though one day in the future you will die physically, in the here and now, you're already dead spiritually. When you stand before God at this white throne judgment, your name will not be found written in the Book of Life, and you'll be cast into the lake of fire. This is the second death.

Revelation 20:6 tells us, "Blessed and holy is he who has part in the first resurrection. Over such the second death has no power." Jesus said, "That which is born of the flesh is flesh, and that which is born of the Spirit is spirit. Do not marvel that I said to you, 'You must be born again'" (John 3:6-7). You've got to have a second birth, a spiritual birth. Born twice, you'll die once. Born once, you'll die twice. You'll die physically and then you'll be cast into the lake burning with fire, the second death, which is eternal separation from God.

But go back a moment. What happens to those who were born again — those who die only once?

They get to experience the encore.

## A RIVER TO FLOW FROM MOUNT OF OLIVES

- Joel 3:18
- Zechariah 14:4, 8, 10

## ALL NATIONS SEE GOD'S GLORY

- Isaiah 60:1-3
- Ezekiel 39:21
- Micah 4:1-5
- Habakkuk 2:14

## ANIMAL BEHAVIOR

- Isaiah 11:6-7; 65:25
- Isaiah 11:8

## CURSE ON CREATION REMOVED

- Genesis 3:17-19
- Isaiah 11:6-9; 35:9; 65:25
- Joel 3:18
- Amos 9:13-15

## DEATH SWALLOWED UP IN VICTORY

- Isaiah 25:8

## ISRAEL AS GOD'S WITNESSES

- Isaiah 44:8; 61:6; 66:21
- Ezekiel 3:17
- Micah 5:7
- Zephaniah 3:20
- Zechariah 8:3

## ISRAEL CLEANSED

- Jeremiah 33:8
- Zechariah 13:1

## ISRAEL ENLARGED AND CHANGED

- Isaiah 26:13
- Obadiah 17-21

## ISRAEL EXALTED ABOVE THE GENTILES

- Isaiah 14:1-2
- Isaiah 49:22-23
- Isaiah 60:14-17; 61:6-7

## ISRAEL RECOGNIZES MESSIAH

- Isaiah 8:17; 25:9; 26:8
- Zechariah 12:10-12

## ISRAEL REGATHERED

- Isaiah 43:5-6
- Jeremiah 24:6; 29:14; 31:8-10
- Ezekiel 11:17; 36:24-25, 28
- Amos 9:14-15
- Zechariah 8:6-8
- Matthew 24:31

## ISRAEL REGENERATED

- Jeremiah 31:31-34; 32:39
- Ezekiel 11:19-20; 36:26

## ISRAEL RELATED TO GOD BY MARRIAGE

- Isaiah 54; 62:2-5
- Hosea 2:14-23

## JERUSALEM, THE HEAVENLY CITY

- Jeremiah 33:16
- Isaiah 2:2-3
- Ezekiel 48:35
- Micah 4:1
- Zechariah 8:5; 14:10
- Revelation 21:10, 16

## JESUS RULES JERUSALEM

- Psalm 2:6-8, 11
- Isaiah 2:3; 11:4

Jesus, the Good Shepherd

- Isaiah 40:11; 49:10; 58:11
- Ezekiel 34:11-16

## KNOWLEDGE OF GOD INCREASED

- Isaiah 41:19-20; 54:13
- Habakkuk 2:14

## LONGEVITY OF MAN RESTORED

- Isaiah 65:20

## MINISTRY OF THE HOLY SPIRIT

- Isaiah 32:15; 59:21
- Ezekiel 36:27; 37:14
- Joel 2:28-29

## NO OPPRESSION

- Isaiah 14:3-6; 49:8-9
- Zechariah 9:11-12

## SICKNESS REMOVED

- Isaiah 33:24
- Jeremiah 30:17
- Ezekiel 34:16
- Isaiah 29:18; 35:5-6; 61:1-2
- Jeremiah 31:8

## SOLAR AND LUNAR LIGHT INCREASED

- Isaiah 4:5; 30:26; 60:19-20
- Zechariah 2:5

## TEARS TO BE DRIED

- Isaiah 25:8; 30:19

## TEMPLE REBUILT

- Isaiah 2:2
- Ezekiel 40-48
- Joel 3:18
- Haggai 2:7-9
- Zechariah 6:12-13

## UNIFIED LANGUAGE

- Zephaniah 3:9

## UNIVERSAL HOLINESS

- Zechariah 14:20-21

## UNIVERSAL PEACE

- Isaiah 2:4; 32:18

## UNIVERSAL PRAYING

- Isaiah 56:7; 65:24
- Zechariah 8:22

## UNIVERSAL SINGING

- Isaiah 35:6; 52:9; 54:1; 55:12
- Jeremiah 33:11

## WILDERNESS AND DESERTS BLOOM

- Isaiah 35:1-2

# HEAVEN

THE DRAMA IS NOW CONCLUDED. In the preceding four acts, we saw the rise of the Antichrist, the rapture of the church, the horror of the great tribulation, the glory of Christ's second coming and the establishment of His millennial kingdom. We saw Satan try to rouse one last feeble rebellion against God, and watched as God squashed that rebellion almost before it began. We saw, at last, the demise of Satan and the judgment at the great white throne. With the conclusion of Act IV came the end of sadness and destruction. But just when you think the curtain has been drawn for the final time, and the last strains of music have drifted to silence, the curtain reopens, and the music begins to swell again.

All good performances deserve an encore. And no performance in history deserves an encore more than this drama of Jesus Christ. There's more beauty to behold, more excitement to discover. In this final section, we will get a glimpse of the glorious future that awaits us in heaven with the Lord. This is an encore that will last for eternity.

## A NEW HEAVEN AND A NEW EARTH

The Scriptures are quite clear concerning the earth and the heavens as we know them now: they will pass away. In Psalm 102:25-26, we read, "Of old You laid the foundation of the earth, and the heavens are the work of Your hands. They will perish, but You will endure; yes, they will all grow old like a garment; like a cloak You will change them, and they will be changed."

Even the universe is subject to the laws of thermodynamics and entropy. The scientist Sir Herschel Jeans described the earth as a great clock that had been wound up and is slowly running down. The sun gives off some one million, two hundred tons of mass every second, but because of its enormous size, you don't have to go home and worry that the sun is going to burn itself out anytime soon.

I heard of an astronomy lecture given once in which the professor said that because of the sun's tremendous rate of reduction, in another ten billion years there will not be enough energy from the sun to support life upon the earth. One half-sleeping student perked up and asked, "What did you say?" The professor repeated, "I said in ten billion years the sun will no longer be able to support life upon the earth." And the student, obviously relieved, said, "Oh, that's good. I thought you said ten million."

In Isaiah 65, the Lord said, "For behold, I create new heavens and a new earth; and the former shall not be remembered or come to mind. But be glad and rejoice forever in what I create; For behold, I create Jerusalem as a rejoicing, and her people a joy. I will rejoice in Jerusalem, and joy in My people; the voice of weeping shall no longer be heard in her, nor the voice of crying" (Isaiah 65:17-19).

The word *create* in verse 17 is *bara* in the Hebrew. It is the same word that is used in Genesis 1:1, "In the beginning God created." *Bara* means to bring out of nothing something into existence. Out of nothing God brought into existence the heavens and the earth. And God is declaring in this passage in Isaiah that He will again create something out of nothing — He will create new heavens and a new earth.

The other Hebrew word for "create" or "make" is *asa*, which means the assembling of existing materials.

Interestingly enough, *asa* is used, for the most part, throughout the first chapter of the book of Genesis as we read of the recreation of the earth in order that man in his present form might dwell upon it. But in the beginning, God created (*bara*) and out of nothing brought into existence the heavens and the earth. Now, God promises He's going to *bara*, or create out of nothing, a new heaven and a new earth.

In 2 Peter 3:10-13, we get a glimpse of how this will transpire. "But the day of the Lord will come as a thief in the night, in which the heavens will pass away with a great noise, and the elements will melt with fervent heat; both the earth and the works that are in it will be burned up. Therefore, since all these things will be dissolved, what manner of persons ought you to be in holy conduct and godliness, looking for and hastening the coming of the day of God, because of which the heavens will be dissolved, being on fire, and the elements will melt with fervent heat? Nevertheless we, according to His promise, look for new heavens and a new earth in which righteousness dwells."

Now, we know a little bit about atoms and the molecular structure. We've come to understand a little about protons, electrons, neutrons, and things of that nature; the basic building blocks of the universe. We know that within the atom are some mysteries that we haven't been able to fathom yet. The nucleus of an atom, of course, is made up of protons clustered together, and electrons that revolve around the nucleus. We also know that in relative terms, there is much more empty space than solid material within an atom.

One of the mysteries of the atom is exactly what holds the protons together. According to Coulomb's law of electricity, like particles repel each other. Protons should push away from each other, and they do push away from each other with tremendous force. And yet, how is it that they are clustered in the nucleus of an atom? Man has learned by bombarding the nucleus of an atom with slow moving neutrons that he can upset the nucleus of an atom and create a tremendous power source. By upsetting and allowing the protons to respond according to their natural bent of thrusting away from each other, the atoms are disturbed to such a degree that the resulting force is atomic power. But as tremendous as that atomic power is, it has been estimated that holding those protons together requires an even greater power than it takes to release them. So the question is, what is holding the universe together?

Paul tells us in Colossians 1:16-17 that Jesus not only created all things, but by Him all things "consist," or, in the Greek "are held together." One day the Lord is going to simply release His grip and the whole universe will instantly dissolve. That's all He has to do — just release His grip and there will be nothing left of the heavens and the earth as we know them. At that point, God is going to create, *bara*, new heavens and a new earth.

## THE NEW JERUSALEM

Think about the most beautiful sites you've seen on earth — places that have not yet been polluted by man. There aren't too many unspoiled places left, but we marvel at the glory of those few untouched sites. Now imagine a fresh new earth, and new heavens, coming from the mind of God, the Master Designer and Creator. Not only will His new creation be unspoiled, it will remain that way for eternity. And He will dwell here with His people.

All of the things that bring pain and suffering will be gone. We will experience absolute joy and bliss as we dwell together with God in His eternal kingdom. Sounds too good to be true, doesn't it? It sounds like a beautiful dream, and yet God has declared it to be true. And His word is faithful. You can count on it.

"Then one of the seven angels who had the seven bowls filled with the seven last plagues came to me and talked with me, saying, 'Come, I will show you the bride, the Lamb's wife'" (Revelation 21:9). John has been invited to observe the new Jerusalem, the City of God. This is the dwelling place of the bride, the place God has prepared for the bride of Christ. Because ours is a God of abundance — a God who forgives abundantly, loves abundantly, and blesses abundantly — we can scarcely imagine the beauty of the place He's prepared for us. But John is given just a small glimpse of what awaits us.

"And he carried me away in the Spirit to a great and high mountain, and showed me the great city, the holy Jerusalem, descending out of heaven from God, having the glory of God. Her light was like a most precious stone, like a jasper stone, clear as crystal" (Revelation 21:10-11). This stone has been translated as jasper, but since jasper isn't clear as crystal, it's possible that this stone, in Greek, is equivalent to a diamond. You know how diamonds sparkle in the light. That's how brilliantly the city will sparkle as you approach it.

Revelation 21:12-16 tells us, "Also she had a great and high wall with twelve gates, and twelve angels at the gates, and names written on them, which are the names of the twelve tribes of the children of Israel: three gates on the east, three gates on the north, three gates on the south, and three gates on the west. Now the wall of the city had twelve foundations, and on them were the names of the twelve apostles of the Lamb. And he who talked with me had a gold reed to measure the city, its gates, and its wall. The city is laid out as a square; its length is as great as its breadth. And he measured the city with the reed: twelve thousand furlongs. Its length, breadth, and height are equal."

Twelve thousand furlongs is approximately fifteen hundred miles. The city appears to be in the form of a cube, with the length, breadth and height all being 1,500 miles in length.

We don't know much about the new bodies we're going to receive. It's going to be fascinating, that's for sure. We can't yet fathom the surprises God has in store for us. 1 Corinthians 2:9 tells us that, "Eye has not seen, nor ear heard, nor have entered into the heart of man the things which God has prepared for those who love Him." We do know that when Jesus rose from the dead, His body was flesh—but He didn't say "blood." He did say that He wasn't a spirit, but it appears that His new body had a different molecular structure because He was able to pass right through walls. Will our new bodies be similar to His? Will our new bodies have mass, or will we be spirit beings? If we're spirit beings, there would be no gravitational pull on our bodies. That would certainly make life interesting.

Now, assuming our bodies do have mass, let's look again at that 1,500 mile cube. On earth, we're limited to the surface space of our planet. But what if we live *within* that enormous cube? Suppose each level of the cube is a mile high and everyone is given one square mile of their own to live in. Do you realize how many people you could pack into that cube? We'd have sufficient room for us all.

> THEN HE MEASURED ITS WALL: ONE HUNDRED AND FORTY-FOUR CUBITS, ACCORDING TO THE MEASURE OF A MAN, THAT IS, OF AN ANGEL. THE CONSTRUCTION OF ITS WALL WAS OF JASPER; AND THE CITY WAS PURE GOLD, LIKE CLEAR GLASS. THE FOUNDATIONS OF THE WALL OF THE CITY WERE ADORNED WITH ALL KINDS OF PRECIOUS STONES: THE FIRST FOUNDATION WAS JASPER . . . (REVELATION 21:17-19).

The foundation of the city will be a colorful, beautiful thing. Jasper, as I mentioned, is clear. So likely, this is referring to a diamond. It is crystal clear, the reflector of light and of color; clean and pure, bright as a transparent icicle in the sunshine.

" . . . The second sapphire . . ." (Revelation 21:19).

The sapphire is blue. This stone is mentioned in Exodus 24:10 as the foundation of God, "And there was under His feet as it were a paved work of sapphire stone, and it was like the very heavens in its clarity."

" . . . The third chalcedony . . . " (Revelation 21:19). Chalcedony is greenish in color. It is an agate and plainly describes it as a variety of emerald gathered on a mountain of Chalcedon.

" . . . The fourth emerald, the fifth sardonyx, the sixth sardius, the seventh chrysolite, the eighth beryl, the ninth topaz, the tenth chrysoprase, the eleventh jacinth, and the twelfth amethyst" (21:19-20). To give you a picture of the colors described here, emerald is green, sardonyx is red, sardius is fiery red, chrysolite is golden yellow, beryl is another shade of green, topaz is greenish-yellow, chrysoprase is golden-green, jacinth is violet, and amethyst is purple. Add to that the brilliant clear of the jasper, the blue of the sapphire, and the emerald of the chalcedony, and you get an idea of the beauty of these gems that make up the foundation of the city.

Gold and diamonds have great value on earth today. They're considered so valuable that men not only work to obtain them, some are willing to fight or even kill to get them. Yet these precious, valuable, earthly commodities will be so common in heaven, we're told the very streets are paved with gold. In other words, earth's treasure will be heaven's asphalt. When we arrive in the new city, it's going to be clear to us that God is not awed by gold, silver, diamonds or precious gems. They're so common to Him, He uses them as building material.

No, God is not impressed with gold, silver, or precious jewels. All the gold within the earth was made by God. All of the silver we have was made by God. All the diamonds, sapphires, jasper, and emeralds in existence are here because God created them. So He's not awed by them the way we are. He doesn't consider them to be a treasure. What the Word tells us — and what we'll see with our own eyes when we enter the city He's prepared for us — is that the thing God treasures is us.

In Exodus 19:5, God refers to His people as His "special treasure." In the King James Version, the phrase used is "a peculiar treasure," and I would be prone to agree with that translation. It's peculiar that God would treasure me. But we are His treasure. It's not gold, or silver, or precious gems that God values. It's His people. More specifically, it's you. He only made one of you, and value is usually determined by the rarity. So you are not only His peculiar treasure, you're His rare treasure.

"The twelve gates were twelve pearls: each individual gate was of one pearl. And the street of the city was pure gold, like transparent glass. But I saw no temple in it, for the Lord God Almighty and the Lamb are its temple" (21:21-22). Now, when Jesus comes for the church and raptures us to heaven, we will find a temple in that first heaven, and it will be exactly like the earthly tabernacle that God instructed Moses to build. When God issued those instructions, He told Moses to be careful to make it exactly according to the plan for it was a model of heavenly things.

We read about that temple in several places in Revelation. Chapter 7, verse 15 reads, "Therefore they are before the throne of God, and serve Him day and night in His temple. And He who sits on the throne will dwell among them." Revelation 11:19 says, "Then the temple of God was opened in heaven, and the ark of His covenant was seen in His temple. And there were lightnings, noises, thunderings, an earthquake, and great hail." Chapter 15:5, 6, and 8 tell us, "After these things I looked, and behold, the temple of the tabernacle of the testimony in heaven was opened. And out of the temple came the seven angels having the seven plagues, clothed in pure bright linen, and having their chests girded with golden bands. . . . The temple was filled with smoke from the glory of God and from His power, and no one was able to enter the temple till the seven plagues of the seven angels were completed."

The temple figures prominently in the first heaven. But in the new heavens, we will have no need for a temple, for God and the Lamb will be our temple.

In the same way, we will have no need for an outside light source. "The city had no need of the sun or of the moon to shine in it, for the glory of God illuminated it. The Lamb is its light" (Revelation 21:23). Jesus said, "I am the light of the world" (John 8:12). In the new Jerusalem, there will be no need for sun by day; no need for a moon at night to reflect the sun. The presence of Jesus will provide all the light we need.

AND THE NATIONS OF THOSE WHO ARE SAVED SHALL WALK IN ITS LIGHT, AND THE KINGS OF THE EARTH BRING THEIR GLORY AND HONOR INTO IT. ITS GATES SHALL NOT BE SHUT AT ALL BY DAY (THERE SHALL BE NO NIGHT THERE). AND THEY SHALL BRING THE GLORY AND THE HONOR OF THE NATIONS INTO IT. BUT THERE SHALL BY NO MEANS ENTER IT ANYTHING

THAT DEFILES, OR CAUSES AN ABOMINATION OR A LIE, BUT ONLY THOSE WHO ARE WRITTEN IN THE LAMB'S BOOK OF LIFE (21:24-27).

Something else that is glorious about the new Jerusalem is that nothing will pollute this city. Nothing will exist of a polluting nature — only things that are pure. In this we will see the fulfillment of Jesus' promise in the Beatitudes: "Blessed are those who hunger and thirst for righteousness, for they shall be filled" (Matthew 5:6).

So often in Scripture, when God spoke of the future and prophesied of things that were to come, He would affirm, "These are true sayings; faithful sayings. I have spoken it. I will do it." I think He made those affirmations because He knew that our imaginations could not conceive of the things He was promising. Since we can't imagine them, we have to take Him at His word. But God is faithful to that Word, and we can, indeed, rely on His promises. Though these descriptions of the new Jerusalem seem "unearthly" (and they are), we can believe that each detail will come into existence just as God has promised in the Scriptures.

When faced with descriptions that are surreal and other-worldly, the question is not "Can God bring these things into being?" The question is, "Will you take

God at His word?" Some people have "intellectual" difficulties believing God. At least, they would say their problem is intellectual. But I think the problem is not a matter of intellect. The problem is spiritual. Jesus was quite blunt about spiritual disbelief. In John 3, while speaking to Nicodemus about the need for each man to be born again, Jesus concluded that God did not send His Son into the world to condemn the world, but that through Him the world might be saved. He then told Nicodemus — very matter-of-factly — "He who believes in Him (the Son) is not condemned; but he who does not believe is condemned already, because he has not believed in the name of the only begotten Son of God. And this is the condemnation, that the light has come into the world, and men loved darkness rather than light, because their deeds were evil" (John 3:18-19).

Disbelief is a moral problem. It's the condition of one who loves darkness so much that they reject the Light. In contrast to that, faith is the natural condition for those who reject darkness and love the Light. In fact, the longer I have walked with Jesus, the greater my faith has become. I have no intellectual difficulty believing what God says. I would have intellectual difficulty in not believing. To try to explain my existence apart from God would be intellectually difficult. To try to explain the fulfilled prophecies of

Scripture presents tremendous intellectual difficulty. But believing God? That's not difficult at all.

Jesus often used the words "verily, verily" when prophesying. The double use is for emphasis. It's as if He were saying, "truly, truly." That tells me He meant what He said. How wonderful that we can count on the truth of God's future plans for the bride of Jesus Christ. Glorious things are in store for the child of God! How thankful I am that I'm a part of God's eternal plan to bestow upon me His love and the glory of His kingdom forever.

## THE TREE OF LIFE

> AND HE SHOWED ME A PURE RIVER OF WATER OF LIFE, CLEAR AS CRYSTAL, PROCEEDING FROM THE THRONE OF GOD AND OF THE LAMB. IN THE MIDDLE OF ITS STREET, AND ON EITHER SIDE OF THE RIVER, WAS THE TREE OF LIFE, WHICH BORE TWELVE FRUITS, EACH TREE YIELDING ITS FRUIT EVERY MONTH. THE LEAVES OF THE TREE WERE FOR THE HEALING OF THE NATIONS (REVELATION 22:1-2).

When God created the Garden of Eden for Adam and Eve, He filled it with a variety of fruit-bearing trees — trees from which Adam and Eve were invited to freely eat. But He also included a tree in the middle of the Garden, from which Adam and Eve were forbidden to eat. This was the tree of the knowledge of good and evil. God warned them that this tree's fruit was deadly. Yet another tree existed in that Garden — the tree of life. The one who ate from this tree would live forever. When Eve heeded Satan's lies and ate of the fruit, and Adam followed her lead, God had to expel them from the Garden and block their entrance back in, "lest he put out his hand and take also of the tree of life, and eat, and live forever" (Genesis 3:22). God's concern was not that Adam and Eve live forever, but that they live forever in that sinful state, the state of rebellion against the commandment of God. Their choice brought the curse of sin into the world, which is yet another thing that will be banished in the new Jerusalem (Revelation 22:3).

You would think with the choice of the tree of death and the tree of life that surely man would choose the tree of life first. But such was not the case. Now, we fault Adam for his folly. Why would he ever choose to eat of the tree of death rather than the tree of life? But before we get too severe in our criticism and condemnation of Adam, we need to realize that the same choice is before mankind today. God has offered to us the tree of life; and that is, of course, in the cross of Jesus Christ, through which God has provided eternal life. And people have a choice today of life and death. In the cross, God said,

"See I have set before you life and death. Choose life that you might live." But even so, there are many people today who choose the path of death rather than the path of life, making the same foolish mistake that Adam and Eve made there in the garden.

From that passage in Revelation, we see that, evidently, that tree of life has been transferred into the city of God. What a picture we're given in Revelation 22:1-2. We see a crystal-clear stream flowing from the throne of God and weaving throughout the city. Beside the stream, streets of gold line the banks. And there, growing strong and straight, is the tree of life — transplanted straight from Eden. We're told it yields twelve different types of fruit, a different type for each month. Not only does it produce an abundant variety of fruit, but its leaves are for the healing of the nations.

What nations does this refer to? We know there will still be an earth. And there will still be nations on that new earth. What kind of people will inhabit it? The Bible doesn't tell. Many things about the future are still to be revealed. God left some surprises for us.

## FACE TO FACE

AND THERE SHALL BE NO MORE CURSE, BUT THE THRONE OF GOD AND OF THE LAMB SHALL

BE IN IT, AND HIS SERVANTS SHALL SERVE HIM.
THEY SHALL SEE HIS FACE, AND HIS NAME
SHALL BE ON THEIR FOREHEADS. THERE SHALL
BE NO NIGHT THERE: THEY NEED NO LAMP NOR
LIGHT OF THE SUN, FOR THE LORD GOD GIVES
THEM LIGHT. AND THEY SHALL REIGN FOREVER
AND EVER (REVELATION 22:3-5).

No more curse of sin. No more night. Just the promise
of a new name, and the reality of reigning forever and
ever with the God who loves us — the God whose face
we shall behold, just as Jesus promised (Matthew 5:8).

THEN HE SAID TO ME, THESE WORDS ARE
FAITHFUL AND TRUE (REVELATION 22:6).

These promises are so glorious, so beautiful, so beyond
our humanly comprehension that for our benefit, God
affirms repeatedly in these last few chapters that He's
telling us the truth. It's not just some kind of a fairy tale.
This is God's truth, revealed to us.

## REWARDS

That would all be enough — the right to reign with
Jesus for eternity, the blessing of seeing His face and
learning directly from Him and living in the glorious
home He's prepared just for us. But in addition to all

that, the Bible tells us that God will reward us for our work on earth.

Salvation is the gift of God through grace. But having received this wonderful gift of God through grace, now that He is my Lord, I am obligated to serve and obey Him. Gratitude is the best motivator of all. Just the remembrance of what Jesus did for us should motivate us to serve Him as an offering of thankfulness. But if we don't serve out of gratitude or thankfulness, we should serve out of obligation. Our lives are no longer our own. Scripture tells us we were bought at a price, and ought therefore to glorify God in our bodies (1 Corinthians 6:19-20). Elsewhere, Jesus asked the obvious question, "Why do you call Me 'Lord, Lord' and not do the things which I say?" (Luke 6:46). That's a complete inconsistency.

We are to obey Him as Lord. And we will each be rewarded according to our faithfulness in doing the things He has commanded. These promised rewards have nothing to do with salvation, but they have a great deal to do with our position in the kingdom of God.

As mentioned in Act IV, Jesus told the parable of the talents in Matthew 25. The master, needing to take a trip to a far country, left his goods entrusted to his servants. To one he gave five talents, to another, four, to another, one. When he returned, he called them in to give an accounting. The one who had been given five talents said, "Lord, I've increased what you gave me. I brought you ten." And the lord said, "Good job. Well done, good and faithful servant. You've been faithful in a few things; now I'll make you ruler over ten cities. Enter into the joy of the Lord." But the one who had taken the one talent and buried it, ended up losing it. He who is faithful in a few things will be given much. But he who is not faithful will lose even that which he was given.

In writing of the judgment of the saints, Paul said, "For we must all appear before the judgment seat of Christ, that each one may receive the things done in the body, according to what he has done whether good or bad. Knowing, therefore, the terror of the Lord, we persuade men" (2 Corinthians 5:10-11). One day, we will give an accounting unto the Lord of what we have done with the things that He has entrusted to us. The Lord is coming quickly. He's coming with rewards in His hand. He's coming for His bride.

AND THE SPIRIT AND THE BRIDE SAY, COME! AND LET HIM WHO HEARS SAY, COME! AND LET HIM WHO THIRSTS COME. WHOEVER DESIRES,

LET HIM TAKE THE WATER OF LIFE FREELY (REVELATION 22:17).

## ARE YOU THIRSTY?

The invitation issued in the verse above makes me think of another invitation which God wrote through the prophet Isaiah. "Ho! Everyone who thirsts, Come to the waters; and you who have no money, come, buy and eat. Yes, come, buy wine and milk without money and without price. Why do you spend money for *what is* not bread, and your wages for *what* does not satisfy? Listen carefully to Me, and eat *what is* good, and let your soul delight itself in abundance. Incline your ear, and come to Me. Hear, and your soul shall live; and I will make an everlasting covenant with you — the sure mercies of David" (Isaiah 55:1-3).

There's no god like our God. In other religions, men must sweat and strive in the hopes that they might reach their god, yet our God left the beauty of heaven to come to us. In other religions, men must make perpetual sacrifice to try to appease their gods. Our God blesses us — abundantly, generously, continually — simply because He loves us.

Are you thirsty today? Perhaps it's because you've spent your money for what is not bread, and your wages for what does not satisfy. If you've looked to the world to bring you joy and satisfaction, you will be left lacking. If you've sought fulfillment through the world's best offerings, you're no doubt thirsting for true beauty. You'll find it only in Jesus Christ.

Throughout the Bible, God's message is simple: "Repent of your sins, follow Me, and obey what I ask you to do." Repentance is more than just being sorry, because you can be sorry for the things you've done and yet go right on doing them. To repent means to have a total change of heart and mind toward God. It means humbly leaving the shallow and empty things in which we have tried to find fulfillment and turning, finally, toward the love and forgiveness of Jesus Christ. This change of heart towards God will give you the power to turn from your wrong and sinful lifestyle. When you experience the goodness of God, you will also experience a genuine desire to change from your sins of the past. You will experience a brand-new quality of life the Bible calls godliness.

The alternative to godliness is, obviously, ungodliness. And that's an apt word for our planet today. We live in an ungodly world, a world headed toward devastation. It is in a spiraling death-dive from which there is no recovery. The signs are all around us — you've no doubt observed them yourself.

As the world has grown darker and darker, God has continued to offer His light. He has not hidden truth from us. Through His Word, God has revealed the path to a meaningful life. He says, "See, I have set before you today life and good, death and evil, in that I command you today to love the LORD your God, to walk in His ways, and to keep His commandments, His statutes, and His judgments, that you may live and multiply; and the LORD your God will bless you in the land which you go to possess" (Deuteronomy 30:15-16). In other words, "If you'll follow My rules, you'll be joyful and prosperous." It's not difficult to understand. But man has hardened his heart, rejected God, and gone after his own way.

The Bible says that the people left on the earth in the last days "did not repent of their murders or their sorceries or their sexual immorality or their thefts" (Revelation 9:21). Another way to say this is that they "repented not of the works of their hands."

This picture of the character of mankind is sobering to say the least. What will people be like at the time of the end? First of all, people will worship devils. God wants us to seek His guidance and His wisdom. He wants to bring direction to our lives. But today people don't seek the counsel of God. Instead they turn to mediums and New Age channelers for guidance. They seek the advice of psychics, fortune-tellers, Ouija boards, and horoscopes. They worship devils rather than God.

The New Age Movement with its growing popularity has brought with it the phenomenon of "channeling," where supposed wise people of the past give their secrets and wisdom to present-day seekers. This is similar to the practices of the oracles of ancient times. In essence, it is no more than demons promulgating their doctrines through mediums, dressed up and made acceptable to modern consumers.

In some public school systems in the United States today, children are taught how to contact their "spirit guides" and receive help from the "wise little man" who "lives in a house in their minds."

Many popular rock groups encourage children to find fulfillment through satanism. Clearly the prediction of widespread worship of demonic spirits is coming to pass.

Not only will they worship devils, but the people of the last days will also worship idols. Everyone bows his knee to some object of worship, some ideal, some principle, some goal, some ambition, or some thing. Every man must worship; this is an innate need. If he doesn't worship

God, then he must and will find a substitute. In Deuteronomy 4:19, the Bible speaks of man literally being driven to worship. It is an inescapable part of our nature.

Christian college students are ridiculed by their secular professors because of their belief in Jesus Christ. Professors make Christians one of their favorite targets, mocking and laughing at those who believe in God. Students are told that man is self-sufficient, with no need for an outdated crutch like faith in God. But then the professor goes home and worships the idol in his backyard — the boat, or sports car, or the garden he's cultivating. Many of these same professors use drugs or are involved in the New Age Movement. They flock to Sai Baba or other gurus who claim to have made the transition into the godhood. Every man has his idol.

Men in the last days will not repent of their murders and sorceries. Millions of babies are murdered each year in U.S. abortion clinics. These murders are condoned and in some cases financed by our government and defended by our courts. God cannot ignore this wanton disregard for life and will surely bring the United States into judgment for it. Perhaps this judgment is already beginning.

Once disorganized, street gangs have now become well-financed and well-equipped purveyors of drugs and violence. We now find addiction and wanton, senseless murder becoming commonplace in every major city in America.

Scripture also tells us that the people of the last days will refuse to repent of their sorceries. "Sorceries" in the original Greek is *pharmakia*, which means "the use of narcotics for thrill or enchantment." Look at the increasingly widespread use of drugs throughout the world today. Marijuana and cocaine are as easily obtained by the youth as candy. These are both personality-changing drugs. The insidious thing about their use is the effect on the brain of the user. These drugs seem to attack the centers of rational judgment so that the user is deceived into believing he is not addicted. An objective observer can see the alteration of personality and loss of good judgment quite easily. The person who is under the influence cannot assess that he is making poor decisions. He hasn't the capability to realize that his ability to make rational choices has been impaired, and is thus trapped. New research reveals that these drugs destroy a chemical in the brain that inhibits the ability to ever resist the drug again.

"Neither did they repent of their fornication." As we look around the world today, we see the lowering and ultimate eradication of any decent standard of morality.

It seems that almost every mass medium of communication is being used to destroy the moral principles that our society and its people once possessed. Immorality has become so pervasive and accepted that people talk freely of their live-in partners as if the practice was of no moral question.

There's so much more. We could go on and on, describing the immoral, ungodly, bleak condition of mankind today. But rather than dwell on the problem, we need to look at the Savior.

Scripture tells us that it is the goodness of God that brings a man to repentance (Romans 2:4). Though we've all been guilty of sin—whether that be idol worship, murder, drugs, fornication, thievery, lying or covetousness—God still loves us. In fact, He loves us so much that He sent His only begotten Son to take the responsibility of the guilt of every wrong thing that we have ever done. Jesus Christ died on the cross in our place so that He could wash us clean from guilt forever.

Some people are so reluctant to change their lives in any way that they think, "I'll just wait until I see God's judgments come upon this earth; then I'll turn to God for mercy." Allow me to speak to you personally. If you don't repent now as the result of the goodness and mercy of God, why would you repent during the time of God's judgments? If the goodness of God doesn't bring you into His family, His judgments are not likely to do it.

Repentance must be the work of God within your life. No person can bring you to repentance. Someone might bring you to sorrow. I might make you feel very sorry, but I can't make you repent. You must allow God to speak to you and touch your heart. Only godly sorrow leads to repentance.

Stop and reflect. Whatever you may be getting out of your favorite sin, is it worth the sacrifice of your soul? Why not turn your life over to Jesus Christ? He has a much better plan for your life today and a glorious eternal future in His Kingdom tomorrow!

Are you thirsty today? Are you thirsty for peace, for hope, for beauty, for righteousness? If so, take a moment in the quiet of your heart to give your life to Jesus. Acknowledge the fact that Jesus, God in human flesh, died on the cross for your sins. Humbly ask Him for the forgiveness and eternal life He so freely offers. I encourage you to do this now, lest you wake up some morning and find the church gone, the world in chaos, and yourself left to face the wrath of God as He closes the door that leads to eternal life.

*Father, we thank You for the wonderful hope You've given us—the glorious promise of Your coming kingdom, where we will dwell together in peace and in love, worshiping You.*

*I pray, Lord, for those right now who are not a part of Your kingdom. I pray that Your Spirit would speak to their hearts and draw them to You. We thank You, Lord, that You've opened the door and invited every man, that anyone who will listen may come in. I pray that those who are weary, those that are heavy-laden, those who are burdened down with the cares of this life, will come to You and submit their lives to you, and find the peace they so long for.*

*Let today be the day, Father, in which many would come into Your kingdom and begin to experience the joy and the blessing of knowing that their sins are forgiven, their hope is secure, and their future is eternal life in Your kingdom, world without end. Draw them, Father, by Your Holy Spirit.*

*In Jesus' name we pray, Amen.*

JESUS STOOD AND CRIED OUT, IF ANYONE THIRSTS, LET HIM COME TO ME AND DRINK.
—JOHN 7:37

# GLOSSARY

**Abomination of Desolation**

This is the action of the Antichrist when he stands in the Holy of Holies of the Jewish Temple that will be rebuilt in Jerusalem. The Antichrist will claim that he is God and call the people to worship him. This is the Abomination of Desolation spoken of in Daniel 9:27 and Matthew 24:15.

**Antichrist**

The term *Antichrist* is a reference to the "Beast" (Revelation 19:20), "Son of Perdition," "Man of Sin," or "Lawless One" (2 Thessalonians 2:1–9). More than any man in history he will be in league with the Devil and do his bidding during the days just prior to the second coming of Jesus Christ. He will be defeated by our Lord when He returns.

**Babylonian Empire**

The Babylonian Empire is the first of four prophetically significant world empires that are prophesied in a dream and vision covered in the book of Daniel.

## Church, or the Bride of Christ

These two terms can be used synonymously to describe all who have received Jesus Christ as their Lord and Savior (Revelation 21:9).

## Common Market (European Union, or EU)

The Common Market or the European Union is an association of certain European nations that many believe will eventually become the final world empire, or the revived and reconstituted Roman Empire.

## Day of the Lord

The Day of the Lord is a phrase often used in reference to a period beginning with the Great Tribulation and ending after the millennial reign of Christ on the earth (1 Thessalonians 5:1–4, 2 Peter 3:1–10).

## Disciples

Jesus said a disciple is one who denies himself, takes up his cross and follows Jesus.

## Eastern Bloc

The Eastern Bloc countries are the countries that at one time lined up politically and militarily with the former Soviet Union.

**Euphrates River**

The Euphrates is a Middle Eastern river that is first mentioned as one of the four rivers running through the Garden of Eden. It is referred to many times throughout the Old Testament and then finally in the Book of Revelation where it is also referred to as the "great river Euphrates."

**European Economic Community**

At present there is a relationship between the various countries of Western Europe that is mostly economic in nature. It has already been determined that member nations will share a common currency, hence it is called the European Economic Community. More recently it has come to be known as the European Community.

**Gabriel**

Gabriel is one of two angels of God named in the Scriptures. He was the angel that appeared to both Mary and Joseph to announce the birth of Jesus.

**Iniquity**

Iniquity is the combination of sins and transgressions.

### Medo-Persian Empire

The Medo-Persian Empire (i.e., the empire of the Medes and Persians) is the second of four prophetically significant world empires covered in the Book of Daniel.

### Messiah

The word *Messiah* means "Anointed One."

### Most Holy Place

The Jewish temple had both the holy place where only the priests were allowed to enter and the Most Holy place (or Holy of Holies) where the high priest would go once a year to offer a sacrifice for the sins of the nation Israel. The desecration of the temple by the Antichrist will precipitate the great tribulation.

### PLO

Palestine Liberation Organization: a political movement uniting Palestinian Arabs in an effort to create an independent state of Palestine.

### Rapture

The Rapture refers to the event where the church is "caught up to meet the Lord in the air" (1 Thessalonians 4:13–18). It is also referred to in 1 Corinthians 15:51, 52.

## Second Coming of Jesus Christ

Jesus often promised that He would someday return. The second coming of Christ will occur at the end of the great tribulation.

## Seventieth "week" of Daniel

The word "week" as used in Daniel 9:27 literally just means seven. This particular seven refers to a seven-year period which will culminate at the end of this present age.

## Sin

To miss the mark. God's mark for us is perfection, anything short of that is sin.

## Solomon's Temple

Solomon's Temple is the temple that the Lord authorized Solomon to build "for Him" to carry out the requirements of worship and service to God and sacrifices made for the sins of the people.

## Son of Perdition (see Antichrist)

## Transgression

Transgression is a term used in Scripture to signify a deliberate, willful breaking of God's law.

## Tribulation/Great Tribulation

The tribulation (sometimes called the great tribulation) refers to seven-year period after the rapture of the church and just prior to the return of Christ to set up His kingdom (Matthew 24:14–30).